NATURAL ENVIRONMENT RESEARCH COUNCIL

INSTITUTE OF GEOLOGICAL SCIENCES

Geological Survey and Museum

BRITISH REGIONAL GEOLOGY

The Midland Valley of Scotland

SECOND EDITION, REVISED

By

M. MACGREGOR, M.A., D.Sc.

and

A. G. MACGREGOR, M.C., D.Sc.

EDINBURGH

HER MAJESTY'S STATIONERY OFFICE

1948

The Institute of Geological Sciences
was formed by the
incorporation of the Geological Survey of Great Britain
and the Museum of Practical Geology
with Overseas Geological Surveys
and is a constituent body of the
Natural Environment Research Council

First published . . . 1936
Second edition revised . . 1948
Seventh impression . . . 1972

FOREWORD TO REVISED EDITION

THE authors wish to acknowledge information freely given by geological colleagues and by others while this Handbook was in preparation. Special thanks are due to the Council of the Geological Society of Glasgow for permission to base Figs. 8 and 10 (both with modifications), and Fig. 11, on line-drawings reproduced in Volume XVIII of the *Transactions* of the Society. The tabular matter on page 45 is also reproduced by permission (with minor alterations) from the same volume.

Fig. 15 has already appeared in 'Economic Geology of the Stirling and Clackmannan Coalfield' (*Mem. Geol. Surv.*, 1932, p. 182). The other Sections and the Maps are all newly drawn. The majority of these are based on the published one inch to a mile maps of the Geological Survey, with later information incorporated in certain instances. Plate VI and Fig. 16 summarize data from various sources.

In preparing the second edition for the press, at short notice, the authors have confined their revision largely, though not entirely, to the selected references listed at the end of each section; these lists have been brought up to date. In most cases the results of research work which have been published since 1936 do not affect the generalized accounts given in the various sections of the original edition—they merely provide additional local detail. The nature of the new work is clearly indicated in the titles of the papers that have been listed; for further information the reader is referred to these publications.

A notable exception to this procedure has been made in the section devoted to Carboniferous palaeontology; since 1936 there have been many changes made in the nomenclature of Carboniferous fossils and the text has been amended accordingly in consultation with experts.

An EXHIBIT illustrating the Geology and Scenery of the district described in this handbook is set out in the Geological Museum, Institute of Geological Sciences, Exhibition Road, South Kensington, London SW7 2DE.

iii

CONTENTS

For a List of References, additional to those of the 'Selected References'
incorporated in the text, see p. 92.

ILLUSTRATIONS

FIGURES IN TEXT

PLATES

PLATE I (*Frontispiece*)

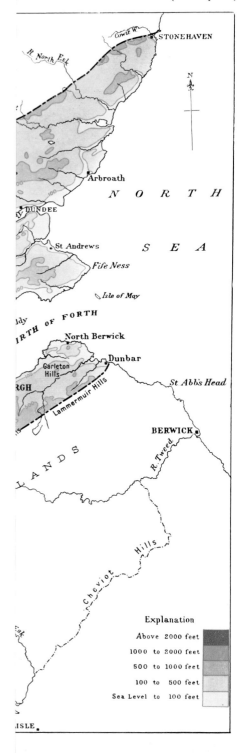

THE MIDLAND VALLEY OF SCOTLAND

I. INTRODUCTION

THE Midland Valley is the name given to the broad undulating lowland tract which stretches south-westwards across the heart of Scotland from the Firths of Forth and Tay to the Firth of Clyde. South of it rises the old tableland of the Southern Uplands, formed of folded Ordovician and Silurian strata, while to the north lies the still higher and more rugged mountain chain of the Grampian Highlands, built up of metamorphic rocks to which, as yet, no definite age has been assigned. The Midland Valley, measuring 120 miles or so in length and about 50 miles in breadth, is defined on the north-west, between Stonehaven and the Firth of Clyde, by the great Highland Boundary fault-line and on the south-east by the Southern Upland fault-line which extends from Dunbar to Girvan. It is thus an ancient rift-valley ('graben') bounded by two parallel dislocations between which the country has subsided, and owes its orientation and form directly to geological structure.

Physical Features. The principal formations entering into the structure of the Midland Valley are the Old Red Sandstone and the Carboniferous. Broadly speaking, the Carboniferous rocks are arranged in a wide compound syncline underlain and flanked by strata of Old Red Sandstone age. The axes of folding are in general parallel to the boundary faults so that a well-marked N.E.–S.W. 'grain' has been produced. In both formations there occur locally great thicknesses of contemporaneous igneous rocks (lavas and tuffs) as well as many intrusions in the form of vents, plugs, sills and dykes. To the differential erosion of these hard igneous masses and the softer sediments among which they lie is largely due the varied scenery so characteristic of the region. The plateaus and ridges of volcanic rocks remain as upland areas while scattered over the whole region are numerous smaller eminences and crags marking the outcrops of intrusions or the sites of volcanic vents. Folding and faulting have also played an important part in the determination of relief while many minor topographic features are due to the effects of glaciation or to the deposits of Glacial and post-Glacial times.

Surface Relief. While the greater part of the Midland Valley (Plate I) lies below the 500-ft. level, considerable areas, especially along its margins, reach a height of over 1,000 ft. and in some cases exceed 2,000 ft. The highest points are Ben Cleugh in the Ochil Hills (2,363 ft.) and Tinto (2,335 ft.) in south-east Lanarkshire.

The main belts of hilly ground extend in a north-east to south-west direction, parallel to the boundary faults. Thus the Garvock, Sidlaw (1,235 ft.) and Ochil (2,363 ft.) Hills, the Campsie Fells (1,894 ft.) and the Kilpatrick Hills (1,313 ft.) form an interrupted belt of high ground stretching from a little south of Stonehaven to the Clyde at Bowling. The first three of these hilly tracts are built up of volcanic rocks of Lower Old Red Sandstone age, the Campsie Fells and Kilpatrick Hills of volcanic rocks of Lower Carboniferous (Calciferous Sandstone) age. Separating this chain of heights from the Grampian Highlands is a well-defined hollow, floored by Old Red Sandstone sediments, which can be followed continuously from the Clyde to near Stonehaven. This feature widens out in the neighbourhood of Methven and Perth into the broad undulating plain known as Strathmore. To the north-west, along the Highland Boundary, the conglomerates of the Lower Old Red give rise here and there to conspicuous heights, as in the ground between Callander and Crieff (*e.g.* Uamh Beag, 2,181 ft.).

The volcanic rocks of the Kilpatrick Hills reappear south of the Clyde where they form the undulating tract of barren uplands between Greenock and Ardrossan, culminating in Hill of Stake (1,711 ft.).

As will be seen from Plate I, a much more interrupted belt of hilly ground fringes the southern margin of the Midland Valley. At the north-eastern end of this tract are the Garleton Hills (600 ft.) formed of volcanic rocks of Calciferous Sandstone age. Some miles to the south-west and on the opposite side of the plain of the Midlothian Coalfield rises the long anticlinal ridge of the Pentland Hills (Scald Law, 1,898 ft.) with its core of steeply-folded Silurian rocks and its coarse conglomerates and thick accumulation of lavas and tuffs of Lower Old Red Sandstone age, flanked by Upper Old Red Sandstone and Carboniferous sediments. At their southern end the Pentland Hills merge gradually into a much dissected area of relatively high ground abutting directly upon the Southern Uplands and extending from near Biggar south-westwards towards Ballantrae and Girvan. The highest points along this tract are Tinto (2,335 ft.) a felsite intrusion (laccolith) of Lower Old Red Sandstone age and Cairntable (1,944 ft.) built up of conglomerates and sandstones belonging to the Upper Old Red. Relatively high ground is formed also by the folded Silurian strata of the Muirkirk-Lesmahagow Anticline (Nutberry Hill, 1,712 ft.) and the Hagshaw Hills (1,540 ft.), by the Lower Old Red granodiorite intrusions of Distinkhorn (1,258 ft.) and Glen Garr with their aureole of baked and hardened sediments (Auchinlongford Hill, 1,340 ft.), by the Lower Old Red felsite intrusions of Glenalla Fell (1,406 ft.) and Garleffin Fell (1,385 ft.) near Straiton, and by the thick teschenitic sills of Permian age intruded among the sediments of the Dalmellington Coalfield (Benbeoch, 1,521 ft.).

The remainder of the Midland Valley falls mainly into two wide undulating plains formed largely of Carboniferous rocks. Much the larger is the broad tract which stretches from near Paisley eastwards and east-north-eastwards to the

Firth of Forth and St. Andrews Bay. South-west of this, and separated from it by the upland area of Calciferous Sandstone volcanic rocks extending from Strathaven to Beith (highest point 1,230 ft.), another and smaller plain lies along the Ayrshire coast between Ardrossan and Ayr. In both, many irregularities of relief are found, the most striking being due to intrusive sheets or bosses of igneous material (*e.g.* the dolerite hills of Fife, the Castle Rock of Stirling, etc.) or to accumulations of Carboniferous volcanic rocks (*e.g.* the Bathgate Hills in Linlithgowshire, Arthur's Seat, etc.). A small area of hilly ground south-west of Ayr is formed of lavas of Lower Old Red Sandstone age (Brown Carrick Hill).

Drainage. Most of the principal rivers that traverse the Midland Valley enter it from the Grampian Highlands in deeply-trenched hollows. This transverse drainage, now flowing across the grain of the country in a general south-easterly direction, represents the relics of an early consequent river-system initiated on an inclined surface produced by regional tilting in Tertiary times. At this period the land stood at a much higher level than it does to-day, and the Palaeozoic rocks of the Midland Valley were perhaps buried under Mesozoic strata. This early river-system has been broken up and profoundly modified by the later longitudinal drainage following the grain along the belts of less resistant strata. Thus the Forth, the Tay and the North Esk retain the old transverse direction through breaches in the line of heights formed by the Sidlaw, Ochil and Campsie hills, but others of the streams from the Grampians have been captured and diverted by the longitudinal drainage of the Strathmore plain. Among the longitudinal or subsequent streams in this part of the Midland Valley are the Isla and South Esk rivers and the Luther Water.

Additional evidence of the early transverse drainage is provided by the passes or wind-gaps that cross the hilly tracts within the Midland Valley itself. Striking examples of these are the wind-gap at the head of Glen Eagles in the Ochil Hills, the Endrick–Carron hollow across the Campsie Fells and the Blane–Glazert depression between the latter heights and the Kilpatrick Hills. Similarly the transverse passes of the Pentland Hills, now occupied by the Lyne Water, North Esk River and Glencorse Water, point to the existence of an older transverse drainage system crossing the tableland from the north-west before erosion had developed the midland plain.

A transverse system of drainage, upon which a longitudinal system has been superimposed, can also be recognized in the fiords and lochs of the Clyde basin. Examples of the former are furnished by lower Loch Fyne, the Loch Eck–Holy Loch depression and the Loch Goil–Gare Loch valley. Cadell was the first to suggest that the drainage of the Dumbartonshire Highlands at one time passed eastwards to the Forth across the Kirkintilloch–Grangemouth depression. This early transverse drainage was gradually disrupted and diverted to the south-west by the development of longitudinal valleys, such as upper Loch Fyne, Loch Long and the Clyde estuary past Arran.[1] The River Clyde itself, which was originally an obsequent tributary of the Forth, was in turn diverted to the western drainage by the opening of the channel past Dumbarton and Bowling.

The evolution of the river-system, accomplished during later Tertiary time, clearly shows how long-continued differential erosion had produced a new orientation of the drainage. Its history is largely the story of the struggle between the older Forth and the younger Clyde for possession of the terrain. By the beginning of the Glacial Period the main features in the physiography of the Midland Valley as we know it to-day had been established.

SELECTED REFERENCES

1865. GEIKIE, Sir A., *The Scenery of Scotland viewed in connection with its Physical Geology;* 2nd Edition, 1887; 3rd Edition, 1901 (Macmillan & Co., London).
1886. CADELL, H. M., The Dumbartonshire Highlands, *Scot. Geogr. Mag.,* vol. ii, pp. 337–347.
1902. MACKINDER, H. J., *Britain and the British Seas;* 2nd Edition, 1907 (Clarendon Press, Oxford).
1910. PEACH, B. N., and J. HORNE, *The Scottish Lakes in Relation to the Geological Features of the Country,* in Sir J. Murray and L. Pullar's *Bathymetrical Survey of the Scottish Fresh-Water Lochs,* vol. i (Edinburgh), pp. 439–513.
1913. CADELL, H. M., *The Story of the Forth* (MacLehose, Glasgow).
1915. GREGORY, J. W., The Age of Loch Long, and its Relations to the Valley System of Southern Scotland, *Trans. Geol. Soc. Glasgow,* vol. xv, part iii, pp. 297–312.
1915. GREGORY, J. W., The Tweed Valley and its Relations to the Clyde and Solway, *Scot. Geogr. Mag.,* vol. xxxi, pp. 478–486.
1930. PEACH, B. N., and J. HORNE, *Physical Features of Scotland in Relation to Geological Structure,* in their *Chapters on the Geology of Scotland* (Oxford Univ. Press), pp. 1–20.
1930. OGILVIE, A. G., *Central Scotland,* in *Great Britain; Essays in Regional Geography* (Cambridge Univ. Press), Chapter xxiii.
1934. LINTON, D. L., On the Former Connection between the Clyde and Tweed, *Scot. Geogr. Mag.,* vol. l, pp. 82–92.
1934. BAILEY, E. B., The Interpretation of Scottish Scenery, *Scot. Geogr. Mag.,* vol. l, pp. 308–330.

Summary of Geology. The tabular statement facing p. 5 provides a synopsis of the geological history of the Midland Valley.

Folding. The Midland Valley is an ancient tectonic structure, probably initiated at the beginning of Lower Old Red Sandstone times. At several periods in its geological history it has been subjected to powerful crustal movements.

(1) The earliest of these took place at the close of Arenig times. In the Girvan–Ballantrae country the Caradocian rests upon an eroded surface of folded and denuded Arenig rocks.

---

[1] Mackinder (1902) suggested that the Tweed "may be the lower course of a river which once had its sources in the Western Highlands," a view which was later adopted and elaborated by Gregory (1915). Such a Clyde–Tweed connection must, of course, have long antedated the Clyde–Forth drainage system referred to in the text.

TABULAR SUMMARY OF GEOLOGY, MIDLAND VALLEY OF SCOTLAND

ERA	SYSTEM AND SUBDIVISION	AREA (square miles)	CONDITIONS OF DEPOSITION	CONTEMPORANEOUS IGNEOUS ROCKS	AREA (square miles)	INTRUSIVE IGNEOUS ROCKS
QUATERNARY	RECENT AND PLEISTOCENE — BLOWN SAND / PEAT / FRESHWATER ALLUVIUM / MARINE ALLUVIUM (Raised Beaches) / SAND AND GRAVEL / MORAINES (terminal and lateral) / BOULDER CLAY (Ground-moraine)		Aeolian (coastal) / Humid continental / Fluviatile; lacustrine / Littoral; marine / Fluvio-glacial / Glacial / Glacial	——		——

PRONOUNCED UNCONFORMITY FOLLOWING EROSION OF TERTIARY TIMES

ERA	SYSTEM AND SUBDIVISION	AREA (square miles)	CONDITIONS OF DEPOSITION	CONTEMPORANEOUS IGNEOUS ROCKS	AREA (square miles)	INTRUSIVE IGNEOUS ROCKS
TERTIARY	——	—	—	——	—	Dykes of Teritary age

MESOZOIC (SECONDARY) STRATA ABSENT IN MIDLAND VALLEY BUT REPRESENTED IN ARRAN

ERA	SYSTEM AND SUBDIVISION	AREA (square miles)	CONDITIONS OF DEPOSITION	CONTEMPORANEOUS IGNEOUS ROCKS	AREA (square miles)	INTRUSIVE IGNEOUS ROCKS
UPPER PALAEOZOIC	PERMIAN .... MAUCHLINE SANDSTONE (Permian lavas below Mauchline Sandstone rest unconformably upon Carboniferous).	20	Aeolian (desert)	Lavas and tuffs	13	Volcanic necks and plugs.
	BEGINNING OF PERMO-CARBONIFEROUS EARTH-MOVEMENTS					Some alkaline basic sills and quartz-dolerite dykes and sills of Permian or Permo-Carboniferous age.
	CARBONIFEROUS — BARREN RED COAL MEASURES / PRODUCTIVE COAL MEASURES / MILLSTONE GRIT / CARBONIFEROUS LIMESTONE SERIES. / CALCIFEROUS SANDSTONE SERIES	104 / 451 / 176 / 744 / 529	Deltaic and estuarine / Mainly lagoonal / Deltaic and fluviatile / Marine; estuarine; lagoonal / Lagoonal	Lavas (local) / Lavas and tuffs (local) / Lavas, etc. (widespread)	554	Some alkaline basic sills etc. Volcanic necks. Plugs, dykes and sills of basaltic and trachytic types.
	OLD RED SANDSTONE — UPPER OLD RED SANDSTONE (Unconformable on older formations) / LOWER OLD RED SANDSTONE (Locally unconformable on older formations.)	375 / 1,511	Fluviatile; lacustrine / Semi-arid; fluviatile; lacustrine	Lavas, etc.	501	Volcanic necks; dykes, sills and stocks of calc-alkaline types.

MAIN PERIOD OF CALEDONIAN OROGENIC (MOUNTAIN-BUILDING) MOVEMENTS

(These movements, which began in Silurian times, were later renewed and folded the Lower Old Red rocks before the deposition of the Upper Old Red Sandstone)

ERA	SYSTEM AND SUBDIVISION	AREA (square miles)	CONDITIONS OF DEPOSITION	CONTEMPORANEOUS IGNEOUS ROCKS	AREA (square miles)	INTRUSIVE IGNEOUS ROCKS
LOWER PALAEOZOIC	SILURIAN — DOWNTONIAN / LUDLOW / WENLOCK / LLANDOVERY	92	Semi-arid; fluviatile / Marine / Marine / Marine			
	ORDOVICIAN — ASHGILL / CARADOC (Unconformable on folded Arenig) / ARENIG	82	Marine / Marine / Marine	Spilitic lavas and tuffs	27	Serpentine, gabbro, etc.

(2) Towards the end of Silurian times began the powerful series of earth-movements which compressed, folded and elevated the marine sediments of the Ordovician and Silurian seas. As a result of prolonged lateral pressure these strata were sharply folded along N.E.–S.W. axes and uplifted within reach of the agencies of erosion. To these movements the term Caledonian has been applied. They were not everywhere contemporaneous. In the Pentland Hills and in Ayrshire the basal conglomerates of the Lower Old Red Sandstone rest on the upturned edges of the folded Silurian rocks while in the Stonehaven district of Kincardineshire the Downtonian rests discordantly upon the Highland Border Series, but passes upwards with apparent conformity into the Lower Old Red Sandstone. There is also an apparent conformable passage from Downtonian into Lower Old Red in the Lesmahagow district. As a result of these movements several N.E.–S.W. depressions were formed, separated by broad tracts of mountainous ground. One of these depressions lay along what is now known as the Midland Valley; another lay farther south along a line now followed by the Merse of Berwickshire and the Solway Firth.

(3) Renewed folding and elevation along the old Caledonian axes preceded the deposition of the Upper Old Red Sandstone. The Lower Old Red Sandstone rocks were bent into anticlines (e.g. Pentland Hills) and synclines and subjected to prolonged denudation. Here and there they were entirely removed and the older formations exposed (p. 30).

(4) Crustal disturbances again affected the region in Permo-Carboniferous times. To these movements, which began towards the close of the Carboniferous and probably continued throughout the Permian, must be assigned the folding, as well as the greater part of the faulting, of the Upper Old Red Sandstone and Carboniferous rocks. This later folding followed, in general, a N.E.–S.W. direction in conformity with the dominant trend imparted to the underlying rocks by the earlier Caledonian movements.

Faulting. The Midland Valley is traversed by numerous faults varying in magnitude from fractures with throws of a few feet up to dislocations with vertical displacements amounting in places to thousands of feet. They fall, broadly speaking, into three groups distinguished by their general direction of strike: (a) a N.E.–S.W. group; (b) an E.–W. group; and (c) a N.W.–S.E. group. The question of the age-relationships of these fault-systems raises, however, many difficulties. Two points should be borne in mind: (a) the crustal disturbances which produced the various foldings to which reference has been made must have been accompanied by faulting; (b) movements have taken place at different periods along the same fault-lines.

The majority of the faults of the N.E.–S.W. and E.–W. groups may be assigned to Permo-Carboniferous times and there is some evidence that certain of the east-west fractures are earlier than certain of the north-easterly group. The faults are, in general, later than the Permo-Carboniferous folding, although in certain cases they appear to be in part contemporaneous. The Permo-Carboniferous quartz-dolerite sills, again, are later than many of the east-west faults (p.74). While therefore folding, faulting and sill-intrusion followed one another, in general, in that order all three must be regarded as roughly coeval.

Most of the N.W.–S.E. faults belong to a distinct system believed to be of Tertiary age. They are certainly later than east-west faults against which they end abruptly. A number of faults with this N.W. trend are, however, merely branches or deflected portions of east-west fractures.

Some at least of the main north-easterly dislocations have had a long and complex history. The boundary faults of the Midland Valley and possibly others with the same general trend were probably initiated in Lower Old Red Sandstone times and their direction determined by the strike of the axes of folding of the Ordovician and Silurian rocks. Later movements along these, or portions of them, took place at different periods.

Along certain of these faults slight movements accompanied by earth-tremors and shocks are still taking place. The Highland Boundary Fault in the neighbourhood of Comrie, and the Ochil Fault, a powerful dislocation running along the foot of the Ochil Hills, are two of the most notable centres of seismic disturbance in Britain.

SELECTED REFERENCES

1924. DAVISON, C., *A History of British Earthquakes* (Cambridge University Press), pp. 62–151.

1942. ANDERSON, E. M., *The Dynamics of Faulting and Dyke Formation with Applications to Britain* (Oliver & Boyd, Edinburgh), pp. 27–54, 86–101, 114–120, 167–183; 2nd Edition, 1951, pp. 29–58, 92–111, 123–130, 179–199.

1951. DOLLAR, A. T. J., Catalogue of Scottish Earthquakes, 1916–1949, *Trans. Geol. Soc. Glasgow*, vol. xxi, part ii, pp. 283–361.

1954. PATTERSON, E. M., Notes on the Tectonics of the Greenock—Largs Uplands and the Cumbraes, *Trans. Geol. Soc. Glasgow*, vol. xxi, part iii, pp. 430–435.

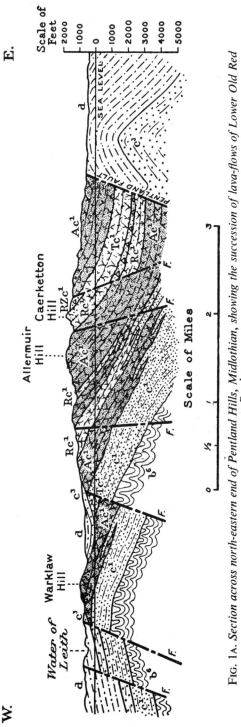

FIG. 1A. *Section across north-eastern end of Pentland Hills, Midlothian, showing the succession of lava-flows of Lower Old Red Sandstone age.*

(For Explanation, *see* Fig. 1B)

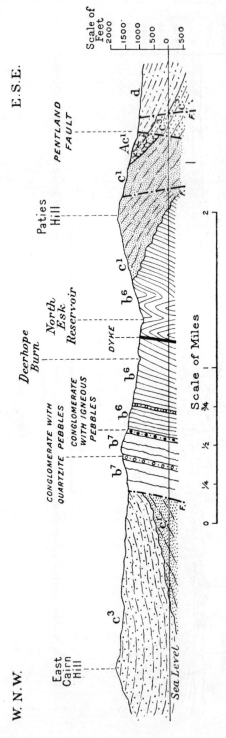

FIG. 1B. *Section across Pentland Hills at the North Esk Reservoir, showing relations of the steeply folded Silurian strata of the Lyne Water inlier to the unconformable Lower Old Red Sandstone*

Silurian: b⁶ = *Ludlow-Wenlock;* b⁷ = *Downtonian; Lower Old Red Sandstone:* c¹ = *sandstone and conglomerate,* Ac¹ = *basalt and basic andesite lavas,* Tc¹ = *trachyte and acid andesite lavas,* Rc¹ = *rhyolite (with trachyte locally);* RZc¹ = *rhyolitic tuff;* c³ = *Upper Old Red Sandstone;* d = *Carboniferous;* F = *fault*

PLATE II.

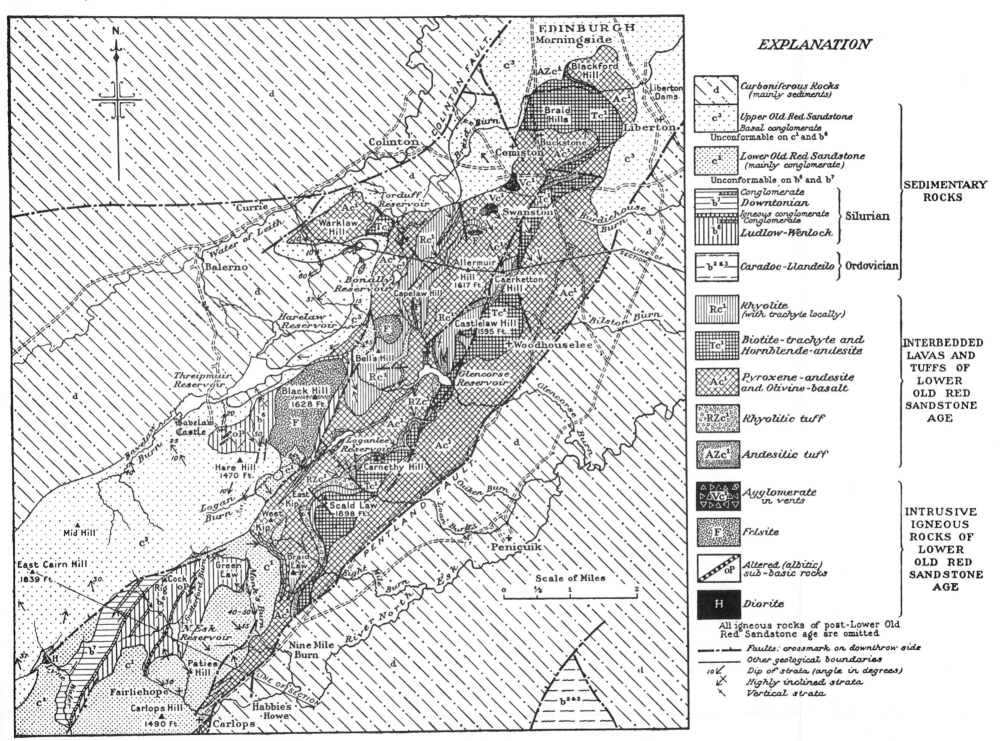

EXPLANATION

d	Carboniferous Rocks (mainly sediments)
c³	Upper Old Red Sandstone Basal conglomerate Unconformable on c¹ and b⁶
c¹	Lower Old Red Sandstone (mainly conglomerate) Unconformable on b⁶ and b⁷
b⁷	Conglomerate Downtonian
b⁶	Igneous conglomerate Conglomerate Ludlow-Wenlock
b²&³	Caradoc-Llandeilo

SEDIMENTARY ROCKS

Silurian

Ordovician

Rc¹	Rhyolite (with trachyte locally)
Tc¹	Biotite-trachyte and Hornblende-andesite
Ac¹	Pyroxene-andesite and Olivine-basalt
RZc¹	Rhyolitic tuff
AZc¹	Andesitic tuff

INTERBEDDED LAVAS AND TUFFS OF LOWER OLD RED SANDSTONE AGE

Vc¹	Agglomerate in vents
F	Felsite
oP	Altered (albitic) sub-basic rocks
H	Diorite

INTRUSIVE IGNEOUS ROCKS OF LOWER OLD RED SANDSTONE AGE

All igneous rocks of post-Lower Old Red Sandstone age are omitted

- - - - Faults: crossmark on downthrow side
——— Other geological boundaries
10↙ Dip of strata (angle in degrees)
↗ Highly inclined strata
✕ Vertical strata

Scale of Miles
0   ½   1   2

MAP OF NORTH-EASTERN END OF PENTLAND HILLS, MIDLOTHIAN, SHOWING VOLCANIC ROCKS OF LOWER OLD RED SANDSTONE AGE AND THE SILURIAN INLIERS OF THE LYNE WATER AND BAVELAW

II. ORDOVICIAN

ROCKS of Ordovician age cover a considerable area on the south-east margin of the Midland Valley in the Girvan–Ballantrae district and appear also in the Craighead–Quarrel Hill inlier on the north side of the Girvan valley. An account of these has already been given in a companion volume in this series of handbooks (Pringle, 1935; *see also* Anderson, 1949). Reference must be made here, however, to three small lenticular inliers of Benan Conglomerate at Big Hill of the Baing, Knockinculloch (north-east of the Pilot) and Linfern Loch, which occur in the disturbed belt of sediments and volcanic rocks of Lower Old Red Sandstone age that adjoins the Southern Upland Fault between Barr and Straiton (Plate IV and Fig. 7). The Big Hill of the Baing outcrop, south-east of Straiton, is the largest, being three miles long. The conglomerate, well exposed in the Water of Girvan near Tairlaw, contains a varied assemblage of igneous pebbles derived from Arenig horizons. At Knockinculloch the conglomerate is associated with Stinchar Limestone and Caradoc shales.

SELECTED REFERENCES

1882. LAPWORTH, C., The Girvan Succession, *Quart. Journ. Geol. Soc.*, vol. xxxviii, pp. 537–666.
1899. PEACH, B. N., and J. HORNE, The Silurian Rocks of Great Britain: Vol. 1, Scotland (*Mem. Geol. Surv.*).
1930. ULRICH, E. O., Ordovician Trilobites of the Family Telephidae and Concerned Stratigraphic Correlations, *Proc. U.S. Nat. Museum*, vol. 76, art. 21, pp. 1–101.
1935. PRINGLE, J., British Regional Geology: The South of Scotland (*Geol. Surv.*); 2nd Edition, 1948.
1935. LAMONT, A., The Drummuck Group, Girvan: A Stratigraphical Revision, with Descriptions of New Fossils from the Lower Part of the Group, *Trans. Geol. Soc. Glasgow*, vol. xix, part ii, pp. 288–332.
1935. REED, F. R. C., Palaeontological Evidence of the Age of the Craighead Limestone, *ibid.*, pp. 340–372.
1949. ANDERSON, F. W., in The Geology of Central Ayrshire (*Mem. Geol. Surv.*), Chapter II.
1952. BAILEY, Sir E. B., and W. J. McCALLIEN, Ballantrae Igneous Problems: a Historical Review, *Trans. Edin. Geol. Soc.*, vol. xv, pp. 14–38.

III. SILURIAN

THE sediments of Llandovery age which enter into the structure of the Girvan–Ballantrae district and of the Craighead–Quarrel Hill anticline have already been dealt with by Dr. J. Pringle in another volume in this series of handbooks (1935, pp. 37, 41–44, 47–48). An account of the Silurian rocks of the Blair, Knockgardner and Straiton inlier (Upper Llandovery and Wenlock) is also given in the same volume (pp. 48–49, 50–51). Farther north-east, however, strata ranging in age from Wenlock to Downtonian[1] occur in a number of inliers along the southern margin of the Midland Valley. These inliers are:

1. Lesmahagow Inlier: ? Wenlock, Ludlow, Downtonian.
2. Hagshaw Hills Inlier: Ludlow, Downtonian.
3. Tinto District: ? Ludlow, Downtonian.
4. Pentland Hills:—
    (a) Lyne Water Inlier: Wenlock, Ludlow, Downtonian.
    (b) Bavelaw Castle Inlier: Wenlock.
    (c) Loganlee Inlier: Wenlock.

Downtonian strata occur also near Stonehaven.

Lesmahagow. The most important of the inliers of Silurian rocks within the limits of the Midland Valley occurs between Lesmahagow and Muirkirk (Figs. 2 and 3) where the following succession has been established:

		Ft.
DOWNTONIAN (about 2,700 ft.)	Red sandstones	1,200
	Conglomerate of quartzite pebbles . .	100
	Red and green mudstones, etc., with Fish-bed	100
	False-bedded red and yellow sandstones .	1,300
LUDLOW (about 1,480 ft.)	Rusty-weathering greywackes, etc. . about	130
	Blue, green and grey shales, etc. (*Platyschisma* beds)	200
	Flaggy, mudstones and shales (*Pterygotus* beds)	350
	Hard grey flags and greywackes, with dark calcareous flaggy shales (*Ceratiocaris* beds and Fish-bed)	500
	Grey, blue and olive shales . . .	300
? WENLOCK	Hard blue greywackes with bands of shale.	1,300

In this inlier the Silurian strata occur in a broad anticline extending for about six miles in a north-easterly direction from the Greenock Water by Priesthill Height and Nutberry Hill to near Lesmahagow. It is only along its north-western margin that the Ludlow–Downtonian sequence shown in the above table can be

[1] The Downtonian of England and Wales is assigned by some authorities to the Upper Silurian and by others to the Lower Old Red Sandstone.

demonstrated, for on the south-east the Ludlow rocks are abruptly truncated by a large fault along which they are brought against different members of the Downtonian succession. The lowest group of the table has yielded few fossils and the scanty palaeontological evidence is not sufficient to determine their exact stratigraphical position. The succeeding (Ludlow) shales have furnished *Ceratiocaris* (two species), *Holopella obsoleta*, *Platyschisma helicites* and a number of lamellibranchs including *Ctenodonta obesa*, several species of *Orthonota* (*O. solenoides*, *O. impressa*, etc.), *Pterinae retroflexa* and *Anodontopsis lucina*. The *Ceratiocaris* beds which follow have yielded five species of *Ceratiocaris*, *Pterygotus bilobus*, *Slimonia acuminata*, fragments of the fish *Thelodus scoticus*, *T. planus* and *Birkenia elegans*, along with *Beyrichia torosa* and a few lamellibranchs and brachiopods such as *Modiolopsis nilssoni* and *Lingula minima* which appear to have no special diagnostic value. The still higher *Pterygotus* beds have furnished numerous eurypterids, including species of *Pterygotus*, *Eurypterus*, *Slimonia* and *Stylonurus* along with species of *Ceratiocaris* and *Dictyocaris*. *Lingula minima*, *Platyschisma helicites* and a few other forms. The distinctive palaeontological feature of the succeeding group of blue, grey and green shales is the abundance of *Playtschisma helicites* here associated with *Spirorbis lewisi*, *Beyrichia kloedeni* (s.l.), *Modiolopsis nilssoni* and several species of *Orthonota* (*O. solenoides*, *O. impressa*, etc.). The highest subdivision of the Ludlow, consisting of flaggy greywackes, has not so far yielded any fossils; its strata are described by Peach and Horne (1899, p. 576) as "merging gradually into the red and yellow sandstones which form the base of the overlying Downtonian." It should be noted that the conglomerate of igneous pebbles which forms the base of the latter in the Hagshaw Hills and Carmichael Burn areas (see pp. 12, 14) has not been detected in the Lesmahagow inlier.

The most interesting band in the Downtonian is the brownish shale, a few feet in thickness, which constitutes the well-known fish-bed. From this horizon came the following fish: *Thelodus scoticus*, *Birkenia elegans*, *Lanarkia horrida*. *L. spinosa*, *L. spinulosa*, *Lasanius problematicus*, and *Ateleaspis tesselata*; associated with these are species of the arthropods *Eurypterus*, *Stylonurus*, *Slimonia*. *Ceratiocaris* and *Dictyocaris*; plant-remains are represented by *Parka* and *Pachytheca*. Sandy shales from a little below the quartzite-conglomerate have yielded *Glauconome*.

Hagshaw Hills. The steeply-inclined strata of the Hagshaw Hills inlier form a well-marked anticline which can be traced from the vicinity of Little Cairn Table north-eastwards by Glenbuck reservoir (Figs. 2 and 3). Along the north-western limb of the arch the strata which have been referred to the Wenlock and Ludlow are followed in upward succession by Downtonian sediments, but the overturned south-eastern limb is truncated by a reversed fault and the Wenlock–Ludlow beds override successive zones of the (generally) inverted Downtonian.

The strata seen consist typically of blue finely bedded shales, grey-blue flaggy shales and hard grey greywackes. The fossils yielded by these beds include: *Favosites asper, Glyptocrinus basalis, Beyrichia kloedeni* (s.l.), *Slimonia acuminata, Ceratiocaris papilio, Calymene blumenbachi, Glassia compressa* and species of *Cornulites, Encrinurus, Proetus, Orthis* and *Orthoceras*. There is little or nothing

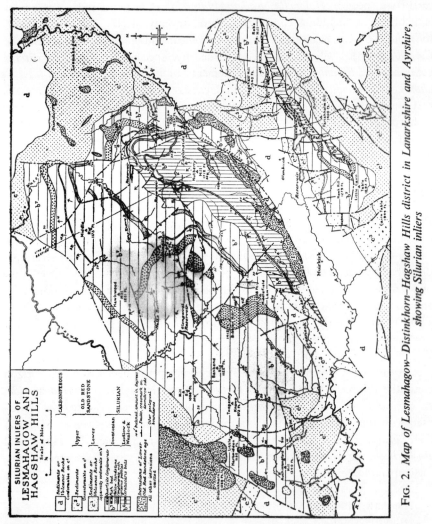

FIG. 2. *Map of Lesmahagow–Distinkhorn–Hagshaw Hills district in Lanarkshire and Ayrshire, showing Silurian inliers*

in this fauna to indicate a higher horizon than that of the Aymestry Limestone of Wales and the presence of strata of Upper Ludlow age cannot be regarded as proved.

Along the northern side of the Hagshaw Hills anticline the Downtonian shows the following upward succession (*cf.* Table on p. 10): (*a*) basal conglomerate

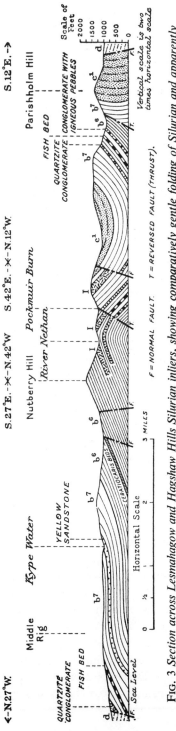

FIG. 3 *Section across Lesmahagow and Hagshaw Hills Silurian inliers, showing comparatively gentle folding of Silurian and apparently conformable Lower Old Red Sandstone*

Silurian: b^6 = Ludlow and Wenlock, b^7 = Downtonian; Lower Old Red Sandstone: c^1 = sandstone and conglomerate, I = intrusive sill; d = Carboniferous.

consisting of pebbles of igneous rocks (Arenig lavas, etc.), chert, and greywacke in a greenish-grey gritty matrix; (*b*) red and yellow sandstones; (*c*) reddish and greenish mudstones with brown carbonaceous shales containing fish-remains; (*d*) quartzite-conglomerate, here 100 ft. or so thick; (*e*) red and grey sandstones overlain by the Greywacke Conglomerate at the base of the Lower Old Red Sandstone. The fish-bed of zone (*c*) has yielded such forms as *Thelodus scoticus*, *Lanarkia spinosa*, *L. spinulosa*, *L. horrida*, *Birkenia elegans* and *Lasanius problematicus* along with species of *Eurypterus*, *Glauconome*, etc. On the south-eastern side of the anticline nothing lower than the quartzite-conglomerate (*d*) is exposed.

Tinto. Two little inliers of Silurian rocks are present in this district, one on the north-west side of the hill around Carmichael House, the other on the south side near Eastfield. Green mudstones underlying the basal conglomerate of the Downtonian at the former locality have yielded *Beyrichia kloedeni* (s.l.), *Dithyrocaris striata* and *Orthoceras dimidiatum*. These and similar mudstones at one time visible at Eastfield were formerly referred to the Upper Ludlow but it should be noted that the occurrence of *Monograptus* in the Carmichael Burn section has not been confirmed. The Downtonian succession is best seen in the more northerly inlier but in neither has any trace of the fish-bed been so far found.

Pentland Hills. The three inliers of this area are enumerated below:

Lyne Water. This inlier (Plate II and Fig. 1B), occupying between two and three square miles of country at the head of the Lyne Water and North Esk River, is the largest area of Silurian rocks in the Pentland Hills. There is an ascending sequence from strata of Wenlock age upwards through beds which have been referred to the Ludlow, into the red sandstones and conglomerates of the Downtonian. Green, grey and reddish shales seen in the North Esk below and above the North Esk Reservoir and in adjoining tributaries have yielded the Wenlock graptolites *Monograptus priodon*, *M. vomerinus*, and *Retiolites geinitzianus* in association with *Phacops stokesi*, *Stropheodonta walmstedti*, *Glassia compressa* and *Trematonotus (Bellerophon) dilatatus*. Of particular interest was the discovery in the Gutterford Burn of a rich eurypterid fauna associated with characteristic Wenlock graptolites; the eurypterids include species of *Eurypterus*, *Stylonurus*, *Drepanopterus* and *Slimonia*; the occurrence of the scorpion *Palaeophonus loudonensis* may also be noted. Among the same series of strata occur certain sandy beds containing well-preserved starfish (species of *Palaeaster*, *Palaeasterina* and *Protaster*) and a thin band of limestone with a rich fauna of crinoids, brachiopods and corals. Among the fossils yielded by this limestone are *Atrypa reticularis*, *Sowerbyella transversalis* and species of *Favosites* (*F. gothlandicus*), *Heliolites*, *Cyathophyllum* and *Cyrtoceras*.

Above these beds come a series of sediments (exposed in the North Esk and its tributaries Wetherlaw Linn, Deerhope Burn and Henshaw Burn) the stratigraphical position of which cannot be so clearly determined. They consist in upward succession of the following zones: (1) hard fossiliferous sandstones and quartzose grits; (2) highly-fossiliferous greenish-grey shales and sandy beds which have provided many species of brachiopods and lamellibranchs, a considerable number of gastropods and a few cephalopods and trilobites; (3) mudstones, shales and sandy bands weathering with a marked concretionary structure; this zone is prolific and certain layers are crowded with *Sowerbyella transversalis*; (4) concretionary greenish-brown sandstones and shales which have furnished, among other forms, *Orthoceras maclareni*, *Camarotoechia nucula*, *Platyceras antiquatum*, *Pterinea retroflexa* and *Conularia sowerbyi*; (5) yellowish-brown sandy concretionary beds overlain by dark-brown sandy shales yielding an abundant fauna; among the commonest fossils found in this zone are *Catazyga* [*Rhynchonella*] *pentlandica* and *Platyschisma simulans* (cf. Lamont, 1947).

Zones (1) to (3) of the above succession may be referred to the Wenlock. Zones (4) and (5) were assigned by Peach and Horne to the Ludlow. But it should be pointed out that there is nothing in the fauna sufficiently diagnostic to prove the presence of Upper Ludlow beds in the inlier, and that there may be a considerable non-sequence at the base of the Downtonian (Jones, 1929).

Both in the Lyne Water and in the North Esk the strata just described are overlain by a series of conglomerates and red sandstones containing intercalations of grey and green shales which have yielded *Glauconome*, fragments of *Lasanius problematicus*, *Ateleaspis tesselata* and *Birkenia elegans*, and other forms characteristic of the Downtonian of Lanarkshire (cf. Lamont, 1947).

Bavelaw Castle. This inlier (Plate II) extends from Bavelaw Castle quarries eastwards towards Black Hill. The beds comprise hard grey shales and flaggy sandstones and grits, resembling lithologically the strata of Wenlock age in the lower part of the North Esk. They have yielded *Monograptus, Retiolites geinitzianus, Glassia compressa, Meristella maclareni* and species of *Orthoceras* and *Dictyocaris*.

Loganlee. This inlier forms a narrow belt of country extending from near Loganlee along the eastern side of Black Hill. The strata, consisting mainly of hard grey shales, are well-exposed at Habbie's Howe near the head of Loganlee Reservoir, a locality which has furnished the following Wenlock graptolites: *Monograptus priodon, M. flemingi* and *Retiolites geinitzianus*.

Downtonian of Stonehaven. The Downtonian of this area (Fig. 4) rests unconformably upon the Cambro–Ordovician rocks of the Highland Border Series and passes upwards with apparent conformity into the Lower Old Red Sandstone. The best sections are those exposed on the coast between the mouth of the Cowie Water and Ruthery Head. The upward succession, as worked out by Campbell, shows (*a*) basement breccias with intercalated sandy mudstones, 200 ft.; (*b*) purple sandstones, 60 ft.; (*c*) grey and brown sandstones with thin red mudstones, 1,000 ft.; (d) volcanic conglomerate and tuffs, 40 ft.; (e) red sandstones, 60 ft.; (f) grey sandstones and fossiliferous sandy shales and mudstones (with fish-band), 600 ft.; (g) tuffs and tuffaceous sandstones, 800 ft. The volcanic conglomerate of (d) is made up almost entirely of rounded boulders of hornblende-andesites and rhyolites. From intercalations of mudstones in (f) come fish-remains now referred to the cyathaspidian form *Traquairaspis campbelli*; the eurypterid *Hughmilleria norvegica*; the phyllocarids *Dictyocaris slimoni* and *Ceratiocaris* cf. *papilis*; the myriapods such as *Archidesmus*.

SELECTED REFERENCES

1868. BROWN, D. J., and J. HENDERSON, On the Silurian Rocks of the Pentland Hills: Part I, *Trans. Edin. Geol. Soc.*, vol. i, part i, pp. 23–33.

1870. BROWN, D. J., and J. HENDERSON, On the Silurian Rocks of the Pentland Hills: Part II, *Trans. Edin. Geol. Soc.*, vol. i, part iii, pp. 266–272.

1882. LAPWORTH, C., The Girvan Succession, *Quart. Journ. Geol. Soc.*, vol. xxxviii, pp. 537–666.

1899. PEACH, B. N., and J. HORNE, The Silurian Rocks of Great Britain: Volume I, Scotland (*Mem. Geol. Surv.*), pp. 527–550, 564–606.

1910. PEACH, B. N., and J. HORNE, in Geology of the Neighbourhood of Edinburgh (*Mem. Geol. Surv.*), 2nd Edition, pp. 10–18.

1913. CAMPBELL, R., The Geology of South-Eastern Kincardineshire, *Trans. Roy. Soc. Edin.*, vol. xlviii, part iv, pp. 930–936.

1925. READ, H. H., Account of Tinto District, in Summary of Progress for 1924 (*Mem. Geol. Surv.*), pp. 96–99; see also *Proc. Geol. Assoc.*, vol. xxxviii, pp. 499–504.

1929. JONES, O. T., in *Handbook of the Geology of Great Britain* (Murby, London), pp. 95–96, 101, 107–108, 112–113, 120.

1935. PRINGLE, J., British Regional Geology: The South of Scotland (*Geol. Surv.*).

1935. STØRMER, L., *Dictyocaris*, Salter, a large crustacean from the Upper Silurian and Downtonian, *Norsk geologisk tidsskrift*, vol. xv, pp. 265–298.

1945. WESTOLL, T. S., A new Cephalaspid Fish from the Downtonian of Scotland, with notes on the Structure and Classification of Ostracoderms, *Trans. Roy. Soc. Edin.*, vol. lxi, part ii, pp. 341–357.

1946. WHITE, E. I., *Jamoytius kerwoodi*, a new Chordate from the Silurian of Lanarkshire, *Geol. Mag.*, pp. 89–97.

1947. LAMONT, A., Gala-Tarannon Beds in the Pentland Hills, near Edinburgh, *Geol. Mag.*, pp. 193–208, 289–303.

1949. LAMONT, A., New Species of Calymenidae from Scotland and Ireland, *Geol. Mag.*, pp. 313–323.

1952. LAMONT, A., Ecology and Correlation of the Pentlandian: a new Division of the Silurian System in Scotland, *Internat. Geol. Congress, Rep. of 18th Session, Gt. Brit.*, 1948, part x, pp. 27–32.

1955. LAMONT, A., Scottish Silurian Chelicerata, *Trans. Edin. Geol. Soc.*, vol. xvi, part ii, pp. 200–216.

IV. OLD RED SANDSTONE

ROCKS of this age occupy considerable areas on both sides of the Midland Valley, fringing and rising up from below the great syncline of Carboniferous sediments. Accordingly they fall regionally into (*a*) a north-western and (*b*) a south-eastern outcrop.

The Old Red Sandstone of the Scottish Lowlands is subdivided into Upper Old Red Sandstone and Lower Old Red Sandstone; the latter is the thicker and more widespread formation of the two, the Upper Old Red occurring chiefly as comparatively narrow outcrops on the inner margins of the Lower Old Red. The junction between them is everywhere an unconformable one.

1. LOWER OLD RED SANDSTONE

This series is most fully developed along the hollow of Strathmore and the Howe of the Mearns (Figs. 4 and 5A). The main structural feature of this tract is the Strathmore syncline, the axis of which passes out to sea a little south of Stonehaven. The sequence as worked out by Campbell for Kincardineshire is as follows[1]:

(5) Strathmore Group: in the Howe of the Mearns consists largely of bright red shales and marls (Edzell Shales; Hickling, 1908) replaced to the west and north by flagstones and massive false-bedded sandstones.

(4) Garvock Group: mainly sandstones and conglomerates in which most of the boulders are of rock-types occurring in the Highland areas; includes also one or two belts of volcanic rocks.

(3) Arbuthnott Group: on the south-east side of the syncline is composed mainly of hypersthene-andesites and basalts with a zone of conglomerates and sandstones at the base; on the north-west side of the syncline these are replaced by volcanic conglomerates and tuffs.

(2) Crawton Group: largely lavas with an underlying series of volcanic conglomerates, tuffs, tuffaceous sandstones and conglomerates in which Highland rocks predominate; the lavas on the south-eastern side of the syncline are porphyritic basalts, those on the north-western side are mainly acid andesites.

(1) Dunnottar Group: the chief characteristic is the extraordinary development of coarse conglomerates with intercalated thin brown sandstones; the conglomerates are composed mainly of quartzites but other Highland rocks also occur; volcanic rocks are found on four horizons.

The estimated thicknesses are: groups (1) and (2), 7,500 to 8,500 ft.; group (3), mainly volcanic, 3,000 to 5,000 ft.; group (4), 3,800 to 4,000 ft.; group (5), at least 1,500 ft. A parallel succession has been worked out by Allan for the country between Tayside and Noranside.

[1] For details of volcanic rocks, see Table, p. 24.

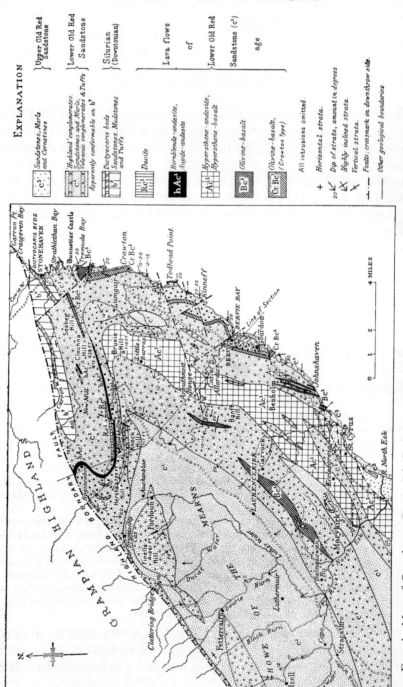

FIG. 4. *Map of Stonehaven–Bervie–Edzell district, Kincardineshire, showing Silurian (Downtonian) beds and apparently conformable Lower Old Red sediments and lavas of the Howe of the Mearns syncline*

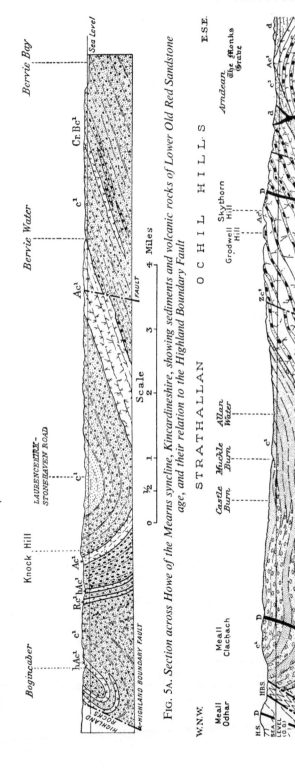

FIG. 5A. *Section across Howe of the Mearns syncline, Kincardineshire, showing sediments and volcanic rocks of Lower Old Red Sandstone age, and their relation to the Highland Boundary Fault*

FIG. 5B. *Section across Strathallan syncline and Ochil Hills showing relationship of Lower Old Red Sandstone rocks to the Highland Boundary and Ochil Faults, and to the Upper Old Red Sandstone and Carboniferous*

Lower Old Red Sandstone: c¹ = sandstone (stippled) and conglomerate (pebble ornament), Cr Bc¹ = olivine-basalt lava, Ac¹ and hAc¹ = andesite and basalt lavas, Rc¹ = dacite lava, Zc¹ = tuff, volcanic conglomerate, etc.; c³ = Upper Old Red Sandstone; d = Carboniferous; H.B.S. = Highland Border Series; H.S. = Highland schists; D = quartz-dolerite dyke; H.B.F. = Highland Boundary Fault; O.F. = Ochil Fault; F = fault

The north-western limb of the Strathmore syncline is steeper than the south-eastern and between it and the Highland Boundary Fault there intervenes to the west of Elfhill (five miles W.S.W. of Stonehaven) a sharp south-west pitching anticlinal fold. Farther west Allan finds the asymmetrical Strathmore syncline truncated by the steeply-inclined reversed Highland Boundary Fault along an axis of monoclinal folding, while north of the Fault the lower members of the Lower Old Red succession lie in a shallow syncline and rest unconformably on the metamorphic rocks of the Highlands.

The main volcanic zone lies, as we have seen, in the Arbuthnott Group. It is well developed in the country north and south of Montrose and again farther south-west in the Sidlaw and Ochil Hills. The lavas of the Sidlaws and of the ground between Glen Farg and Tayport on the south side of the Firth of Tay are arranged in a broad arch, the centre of which has been denuded away along Lower Strath Earn and the Carse of Gowrie to expose the underlying sediments. In the Ochil Hills the volcanic rocks, estimated to be over 6,500 ft. thick, lie almost entirely on the north-western limb of the arch, the south-eastern limb being cut out by the Ochil Fault, and are succeeded to the north by the great series of sediments, sandstones, shales, flagstones and conglomerates, occupying the Strathmore hollow (Fig. 5B).

A feature of the Lower Old Red sediments of the region is the extraordinary development of coarse conglomerates; these fall, broadly speaking, into three groups. The lowest group is characterized by the abundance of Highland rocks; quartzites are the commonest rock-types represented but boulders of jasper, chert, grit, etc., derived from the Highland Border Series, are also numerous and indicate that in early Lower Old Red times these Highland Border rocks must have had a wide extension over the Eastern Highlands. The middle group of conglomerates is composed mainly of volcanic rocks (lava-conglomerates) while in the upper group boulders and pebbles of quartzite and flaggy gneiss preponderate.

Along the south-western outcrop again igneous rocks bulk largely in the sequence. In the Pentland Hills (Plate II) the basement conglomerates and sandstones are succeeded by a great thickness of lavas with subordinate bands of ash and occasional intercalations of sedimentary material (Table, p. 24). A very similar succession holds for the country round Tinto where the volcanic rocks are followed by sandstones containing bands of lava-conglomerate. In both areas the base of the Series is defined by a conglomerate made up of pebbles of greywacke, chert, jasper, etc., derived from the Silurian rocks of the Southern Uplands (*Greywacke Conglomerate*). The general succession thus is:

(3) Sandstones and conglomerates, with bands of lava-conglomerate.
(2) Volcanic rocks with sedimentary intercalations.
(1) Sandstones, chocolate-coloured or brownish, with conglomerates; Greywacke Conglomerate at base.

A. OCHIL HILLS FROM STIRLING CASTLE

(For explanation, *see* p. vii.)

B. ARTHUR'S SEAT AND SALISBURY CRAIGS, EDINBURGH, FROM THE SOUTH

(For explanation, *see* p. vii.)

The sandstones of group (1) cover a large area in the Lanark–Lesmahagow country and are exposed in the gorges of the Upper Clyde above and below Lanark (Bonnington, Cora Linn, Stonebyres); they extend westwards to the slopes of Distinkhorn (Fig. 6) where their thickness is estimated to be about 2,200 ft. and where they are overlain by the volcanic rocks of group (2). The same two groups are present also farther south-west, along the Southern Upland Fault between Dalleagles and Barr, and cover a considerable area in south-central Ayrshire around Kirkoswald, Maybole and Dunure.

Types of Sediment. The main types of sediment are as follows:
Sandstones. These are, as a rule, somewhat soft and gritty but sometimes fine-grained and hard. The prevalent tints are dull red, reddish-brown or bright red, but locally they may be greenish or yellowish-brown. They often contain a considerable proportion of feldspar grains, of black or white mica, and of other grains probably derived as disintegration products from igneous rocks.

Flaggy sandstones and *flagstones* occur on several horizons; the flagstones have been locally quarried (Carmyllie, etc.) for building and paving purposes.

Bright red *marls* and variously tinted, often mottled, *shales* are characteristic of the higher beds present in the Strathmore syncline.

Conglomerates and *grits.* Conglomerates are very abundant in the Lower Old Red Sandstone of the Midland Valley and are specially characteristic of the lower part of the Series.

Conditions of Deposition. Certain characteristic features of the lava-flows have long been known through the writings of Sir Archibald Geikie. Within the Midland Valley these features are finely displayed in the coast sections of Kincardineshire and Ayrshire; they are equally characteristic of the lavas of Lower Old Red Sandstone age in the Lorne and Glen Coe areas of the Western Highlands. Fine-grained sediment is everywhere bedded down into cracks and cavities to form veins and pockets in the lavas, and occasionally gives rise to lenticular intercalations between the flows. At many horizons the lavas are associated with, or separated by, thick bands of conglomerate composed of pebbles of lava and of local sedimentary rocks of pre-Lower Old Red Sandstone age.

Geikie believed that the lavas flowed out under and into water, from vol-canoes that rose as islands above the fresh waters of his 'Lake Caledonia'; the agglomerates he regarded as shingle beaches. A more probable hypothesis regarding the physical conditions of Lower Old Red Sandstone time*was initiated by Bonney and has been gradually developed during the present century; it may be summarized in the following paragraph.

The Lower Old Red Sandstone of the Midland Valley was formed under semi-arid conditions in a wide depression between the Highland Boundary and

Southern Upland Faults. The conglomerates interbedded with the sandstones were laid down as torrential gravels or boulder deposits swept outwards from the Highland Mountains and the Southern Uplands on to the floor of the depression; the sandstones were partly fluviatile and partly formed in temporary lakes. The lavas were erupted from volcanoes that arose along the flanks of the mountains and on the fluviatile and lacustrine plain, and were essentially sub-aerial in character, though some may have flowed into shallow water. Pillow-structure is, however, quite unknown in the lavas. Fine sediment was washed by rain or floods into cracks or cavities and settled in temporary shallow pools on the lava tops. In these deposits the footprints and tracks of small animals have been locally preserved. The volcanic conglomerates intercalated in the lavas were formed as torrential deposits, their pebbles being often largely the products of contemporaneous denudation of local flows.

PALAEONTOLOGY

Most of the fossil-remains recorded from the Lower Old Red Sandstone of the Midland Valley come from Kincardineshire or Forfarshire (Angus). The chief fossil localities in Kincardineshire are those of Canterland Den (Den of Morphie: Garvock Group), and Three Wells near Bervie (Arbuthnott Group); and in Forfarshire those of Turin Hill, Carmyllie, Ferryden, Balruddery, Newtyle, Leysmill and Farnell. Fish-remains are represented by *Ischnacanthus gracilis, Thelodus pagei, Parexus incurvus, Climatius scutiger* and *Cephalaspis lyelli,* recorded from both counties; and by the following forms obtained from localities in Forfarshire: *Mesacanthus mitchelli, Parexus falcatus, Pteraspis mitchelli, Climatius reticulatus, C. macnicoli, Farnellia tuberculata* and *Protodus scoticus.* From Forfarshire also come the following eurypterids: *Pterygotus minor, Stylonurus scoticus, S. ensiform, S. powriei* and *Eurypterus brewsteri. Pterygotus anglicus* has been obtained from both counties. Myriapods are represented by *Kampecaris forfarensis* and *Archidesmus macnicoli.*

Pterygotus anglicus, Kampecaris forfarensis, Climatius scutiger and *Ischna-canthus gracilis* have been recorded, along with a few other forms, from localities in Fife.

Cephalaspis lyelli occurs in the Distinkhorn sandstones of Penning Hill, south-east of Darvel, Ayrshire. *Kampecaris tuberculata,* collected by John Smith from sediments between lava-flows, near Dunure, has been described and figured in *Proc. Roy. Physical Soc. Edinburgh,* vol. xx, 1923, pp. 277–280.

A few plant-remains have been recorded. *Zosteropyllum myretonianum* is common in the Arbroath and Carmyllie Flagstones, associated with *Pachytheca, Parka decipiens,* and *Nematophyton forfarensis.* The sandstones and mudstones of the higher Strathmore beds have yielded *Arthrostigma gracile, Psilophyton princeps* and *Pachytheca sp.*

SELECTED REFERENCES (STRATIGRAPHY AND PALAEONTOLOGY)

1883. PEACH, B. N., On Some Fossil Myriapods from the Lower Old Red Sandstone of Forfarshire, *Proc. Roy. Physical Soc. Edin.*, vol. vii, pp. 177–188.
1908. HICKLING, G., The Old Red Sandstone of Forfarshire, *Geol. Mag.*, pp. 396–402.
1909. SMITH, J., Upland Fauna of the Old Red Sandstone Formation of Carrick, Ayrshire (Cross, Kilwinning).
1912. CRAIG, R. M., and D. BALSILLIE, The Geology of the Country around Dundee, *Brit. Assoc. Handbook*, Dundee, pp. 538–545, 547–551.
1912. HICKLING, G., The Old Red Sandstone Rocks near Arbroath, *Proc. Geol. Assoc.*, vol. xxiii, pp. 299–301.
1912. HICKLING, G., On the Geology and Palaeontology of Forfarshire, *ibid.*, pp. 302–311.
1913. CAMPBELL, R., The Geology of South-Eastern Kincardineshire, *Trans. Roy. Soc. Edin.*, vol. xlviii, part iv, pp. 923–960; see also *Proc. Geol. Assoc.*, vol. xxiii, 1912, pp. 291–298.
1915. DON, A. W. R., and G. HICKLING, On Parka Decipiens, *Quart. Journ. Geol. Soc.*, vol. lxxi, pp. 648–666.
1925. READ, H. H., Account of Tinto District, in Summary of Progress for 1924 (*Mem. Geol. Surv.*), pp. 96–103.
1926. LANG, W. H., On the Identification of the large 'Stems' in the Carmyllie Beds of the Lower Old Red Sandstone as *Nematophyton*, *Trans. Roy. Soc. Edin.*, vol. liv, part iii, pp. 792–799.
1928. ALLAN, D. A., The Geology of the Highland Border from Tayside to Noranside, *Trans. Roy. Soc. Edin.*, vol. lvi, part i, pp. 57–88.
1932. LANG, W. H., On Arthrostigma, Psilophyton and some associated Plant-remains from the Strathmore Beds of the Caledonian Lower Old Red Sandstone, *Trans. Roy. Soc. Edin.*, vol. lvii, part ii, pp. 491–521.
1940. ALLAN, D. A., The Geology of the Highland Border from Glen Almond to Glen Artney, *Trans. Roy. Soc. Edin.*, vol. lx, part i, pp. 171–193.
1947. ANDERSON, J. G. C., The Geology of the Highland Border: Stonehaven to Arran, *Trans. Roy. Soc. Edin.*, vol. lxi, part ii, pp. 479–515.
See also Geological Survey Memoirs (p. 94) on Fife, Neighbourhood of Edinburgh, Glasgow District, North Ayrshire, and Central Ayrshire.

IGNEOUS ROCKS: PETROLOGY

Volcanic rocks of Lower Old Red Sandstone age (p. 21) form extensive areas of relatively high relief in the Midland Valley of Scotland (p. 2). Along with the volcanic rocks are found a few ash necks, sills and dykes of various petrographical types, and one or two small masses of granodiorite and diorite.

The Midland Valley in Lower Old Red Sandstone times formed part of a well-marked petrographical province, extending into the Highlands and the Southern Uplands, in which all the igneous rocks belong to the calc-alkaline magma series.

Among the lavas and tuffs acid types at more than one horizon are preceded and followed by basic in all the districts where they occur. Where acid lavas are absent, acid sills may cut basic lavas but be cut in turn by basic dykes (Tairlaw, south of Straiton).

LOCAL SEQUENCES OF VOLCANIC ROCKS OF LOWER OLD RED SANDSTONE AGE

Brown Carrick Hill Area N. of (Maybole, Ayrshire)	Pentland Hills (Midlothian)	Highland Border (Tayside to Noranside)	Kincardineshire
Upper Old Red Sandstone UNCONFORMITY	*Upper Old Red Sandstone* UNCONFORMITY	*Sandstones and conglomerates.*	*Sandstones, etc.*
4. Porphyritic hypersthene-andesites and olivine-basalts.	8. Olivine-basalts and basic andesites. (Carnethy and Hillend Group.)	9. Olivine-basalt.	*Highland conglomerates.* 9. Olivine-basalts (Garvock Group).
3. Augite-andesite with few or no phenocrysts (local).	7. Acid biotite-andesites and biotite-trachytes (Woodhouselee and Braid Hills Group).	8. Porphyritic pyroxene-andesites. FAULT	*Highland conglomerates.* 8. Olivine-basalts (Garvock Group).
2. Mainly porphyritic olivine-basalts.	6. Rhyolite lavas and tuffs (Caerketton Group).	7. { Microporphyritic hypersthene-andesites and olivine-basalts. *Volcanic conglomerate.*	*Highland conglomerates.* 7. { Hypersthene-andesites and olivine-hypersthene-basalts (Arbuthnott Group).
1. { Olivine-rich basalts, with (locally) a flow of augite-andesite with few or no phenocrysts. *Conglomerates.* *Sandstones.*	5. Basic andesites and olivine-basalts (Allermuir Group).	6. Biotite-andesite.	6. Olivine-basalts (Arbuthnott Group).
	4. Rhyolite (Allermuir Group).	5. Olivine-basalts.	*Highland or volcanic conglomerates and tuffs.*
	3. Basic andesites and olivine-basalts (Allermuir Group).	4. Dacite.	5. { Olivine-basalts (mainly porphyritic) or (locally) hornblende- and augite-andesites, olivine-basalts and dacite (Crawton Group). *Volcanic and Highland conglomerates, tuffs, etc.*
	2. Rhyolites, some trachytes, and subordinate conglomerate (Bell's Hill and Howden Burn Group).	3. Biotite-andesites.	4. Olivine-basalts (Dunnottar Group).
	1. Olivine-basalts and basic andesites (Bonally Group).	2. Olivine-basalt.	3. Acid tuffs (Dunnottar Group). *Conglomerate.*
		1. Pyroxene-andesite. *Conglomerates, sandstones and tuffs.*	2. { Tuffs, and one flow of augite-andesite (Dunnottar Group). *Volcanic conglomerates, tuffs and sandstones.*
			1. Acid tuffs (Dunnottar Group). *Volcanic and Highland conglomerates.*

TABLE SHOWING MINERAL CONSTITUENTS OF IGNEOUS ROCKS OF LOWER OLD RED SANDSTONE AGE

ROCK NAME	PHENOCRYSTS or PORPHYRITIC CRYSTALS. (Relatively large crystals set in a matrix of much smaller ones)	GROUNDMASS or matrix of porphyritic rocks; or FABRIC of non-porphyritic rocks	REMARKS	MODE OF OCCURRENCE
RHYOLITE	Alkali feldspar, biotite. *Some types non-porphyritic.*	Sanidine, albitic plagioclase, quartz; sparse iron-ore and apatite. More quartz than in trachytes. Spherulitic structure may occur.	Alkali feldspar phenocrysts sanidine or albitic plagioclase. Flow structure often brought out by colour-banding. Silicified trachytes may be indistinguishable from rhyolites.	
TRACHYTE	Alkali feldspar, biotite. *Some types almost non-porphyritic.*	Alkali feldspar, quartz; sparse iron-ore and apatite.		
DACITE	Quartz, feldspar, biotite.	Mainly albitic or potash feldspar and quartz.	Feldspar phenocrysts often albitic plagioclase and sanidine. Flow structure common.	LAVA FLOWS
BIOTITE- AND HORNBLENDE-ANDESITE	Plagioclase feldspar, biotite, or hornblende. *Some types almost non-porphyritic.*	Oligoclase or andesine, biotite or hornblende, iron-ore, apatite.	Plagioclase phenocrysts andesine. Flow structure common.	
PYROXENE-ANDESITE	Plagioclase feldspar hypersthene and/or augite. *Some types almost non-porphyritic.*	Oligoclase or andesine, pyroxene, iron-ore, apatite. Mesostasis of glass or alkaline feldspar full of iron-ore dust.	Plagioclase phenocrysts andesine or labradorite. Flow structure may occur. Rocks often very fresh.	
BASALT	Plagioclase feldspar, olivine, augite or rhombic pyroxene. *Plagioclase, pyroxene, or almost all phenocrysts may be absent.*	Andesine or labradorite, pyroxene, olivine, iron-ore, apatite. Biotite scraps if alkaline feldspar present (*e.g.* as mesostasis full of iron-ore dust).	Plagioclase phenocrysts labradorite. Rhombic pyroxenes enstatite or hypersthene. Flow structure may occur.	
FELSITE	Alkali feldspar, biotite (sparse quartz). *Some types almost non-porphyritic.*	Alkali feldspar, quartz, sparse iron-ore.	Alkali feldspar phenocrysts often albitic plagioclase. Flow structure may occur.	
QUARTZ-PORPHYRY	Quartz, alkali feldspar, biotite.	Alkali feldspar, quartz, sparse iron-ore.	Alkali feldspar phenocrysts often albitic plagioclase.	
ACID PORPHYRITE	Plagioclase feldspar, biotite or hornblende.	Plagioclase, sparse ferromagnesian grains, alkali feldspar, sparse quartz, iron-ore, apatite.	Plagioclase usually looks albitized; original composition doubtful. Flow structure may occur.	
PLAGIOPHYRE	*Phenocrysts* (albitized plagioclase and ferromagnesian pseudomorphs) *sparse and small, or absent.*	Albitic plagioclase, pyroxene or hornblende, orthoclase, quartz, iron-ore, apatite.	A vague term for highly altered sparsely porphyritic andesitic rocks with albitic feldspars. Flow structure may occur.	INTRUSIONS: DYKES, SILLS or LACCOLITHS
PORPHYRITE	Plagioclase feldspar, pyroxene (augite or hypersthene) or hornblende.	Andesine, less basic feldspar, pyroxene or hornblende, iron-ore, apatite.	Plagioclase phenocrysts labradorite or andesine. Flow structure may occur.	
MICRODIORITE	*Phenocrysts* (plagioclase feldspar) *very sparse or absent.*	Andesine-labradorite, less basic feldspar, pyroxene, quartz, iron-ore, apatite.	Plagioclase phenocrysts andesine or labradorite.	
KERSANTITE	*No true phenocrysts, but pyroxenes and olivines vary much in size.*	Oligoclase-andesine, sodic alkali feldspar biotite pyroxene, olivine, quartz, iron-ore, apatite.	A variety of lamprophyre. A rare type (Ayrshire).	
DOLERITIC PORPHYRITE	Plagioclase feldspar (very numerous).	Andesine or labradorite, pyroxene, quartzo-feldspathic residuum, iron-ore, apatite.	Plagioclase phenocrysts andesine or labradorite.	
QUARTZ-DOLERITE	*Phenocrysts* (plagioclase feldspar) *usually absent.*	Labradorite, less basic feldspar, quartz, hypersthene and/or augite, iron-ore, apatite; (olivine, biotite).	Plagioclase phenocrysts acid labradorite.	
DOLERITE	None.	Labradorite, augite, olivine, iron-ore, apatite; (biotite).		
DIORITE	None.	Plagioclase, orthoclase (sparse), quartz, pyroxene, hornblende, biotite, iron-ore, sphene, apatite.	Plagioclase albite-oligoclase to acid labradorite. Hornblende usually replaces original pyroxene.	INTRUSIONS: SMALL STOCKS or BOSSES.
GRANODIORITE	None.	Plagioclase, soda-orthoclase, quartz, hornblende, biotite, iron-ore, sphene, apatite.	Plagioclase albite-oligoclase to andesine. Confined to Ayrshire-Lanarkshire border.	

Note. Plagioclase feldspars are very commonly albitized. Alteration products usually present are chlorite and calcite (in most types of rock) and kaolin and quartz (*e.g.* in rhyolites and trachytes)

There is little doubt that all the dioritic and granodioritic intrusions are younger than the lavas, although this cannot be proved in every instance (*e.g.* Distinkhorn). In Ayrshire diorites and granodiorites are younger than many of the dykes and small sills, but older than others.

Olivine-basalt Lavas. It seems clear from the more recent published accounts that a large proportion, probably the majority, of the lava-flows are olivine-bearing rocks: these flows may be non-porphyritic, or they may carry phenocrysts of olivine or pyroxene along with acid and medium labradorite, the latter being often very abundant. Such porphyritic rocks may have basic andesine or labradorite as the groundmass feldspar, and they have been called basic andesites by some authors and basalts by others. We shall refer to them here as basalts, in order to distinguish them from the olivine-free pyroxene-andesites, which also have a wide distribution.

Olivine-basalts have been recorded from all districts, with the exception of the Broughty Ferry area near Dundee, porphyritic types being most prevalent. Among the latter may be mentioned the well-known 'Carnethy Porphyry' of the Pentland Hills, and the very similar basalt of Crawton Type from Kincardine-shire.

An olivine-basalt lava at Friarton Hill, Perth, is quite abnormal in containing some analcite in segregation veins (Davidson, 1932).

Andesite Lavas. *Pyroxene-andesites*, including *hypersthene-andesites*, come next in abundance: they have a similar wide distribution, but are absent or very scarce near Lunan Bay south of Montrose, in the Sidlaw Hills near Perth, and in the Dalmellington–Straiton area. *Hornblende-andesites*, usually accompanied by *biotite-andesites*, are found at certain horizons between the River Tay and the Noran Water, in Kincardineshire, in the Pentland Hills, in the Biggar–Tinto district, and near Corsoncone Hill east of New Cumnock.

Acid Lavas. *Dacites* have been recognized locally between the River Tay and the Noran Water ('Lintrathen Porphyry'), in Kincardineshire and in the Ochil Hills.

Trachytes and *rhyolites* occur at more than one horizon in the Pentland Hills district, and near Biggar and Tinto.

Agates or ' **Scotch Pebbles.**' Silica in various forms is the characteristic amygdale mineral filling the vesicles (gas-cavities) of Midland Valley lava-flows of Lower Old Red Sandstone age. Being harder than the lavas in which they occur, the silica amygdales weather out of their matrix to form pebbles. These 'Scotch Pebbles' have long been collected from river-gravels, and from the shingle beaches of Ayrshire and Kincardineshire, and polished for use as semi-precious stones. The silica of the amygdales may be wholly or partly in the form of concentrically-banded agate, parallel-banded onyx, jasper, rock-crystal, amethyst, etc. Amygdales composed of calcite or chloritic material ('green earth') are also found.

C

A suite of Ayrshire agates has been described in a well-illustrated monograph (Smith, 1910), and selected specimens are exhibited in the Geological Museum in London. The beautiful Thoms Collection of Scottish agates (Heddle, 1901) may be seen in the Royal Scottish Museum, Edinburgh.

Tuffs. Normal bedded tuffs are on the whole very scarce among the lava-flows, except perhaps in the western Ochils, but volcanic conglomerates, largely composed of well-rounded andesitic and basaltic lava-pebbles in an ashy matrix, are everywhere very characteristic. On published maps these ashy conglomerates are shown in some cases as sediments, in others as tuffs.

Acid tuffs, composed of fragments of acid andesitic or rhyolitic rocks, are found locally in Kincardineshire, in the Pentland Hills, at West Linton, at Tairlaw Ring (east of Garleffin Fell), and on the coast west of Maybole.

Volcanic Necks. Vents, wholly or partly filled with agglomerate, have been recognized only in the Pentland Hills, and near Tincorn Hill, Dalmellington and Maybole. Mochrum Hill, near Maybole, is the best example, and stands up as a prominent landmark.

Felsites, etc. The more acid types, such as *felsite, quartz-porphyry* and *acid porphyrite* are the most abundant of the intrusive rocks. In the north they are represented only by sporadic dykes and by a few intrusions in the western Ochils and near Dundee. Near the Southern Upland Fault, however, they form numerous thick laccolithic sills and smaller sheets, and have been extensively quarried for road-metal, especially at Muirkirk, Lesmahagow and Tinto. These rocks offer great resistance to weathering agencies and form such prominent heights as Black Hill (Pentlands), Tinto (near Biggar), Garleffin Fell and Glenalla Fell (near Straiton).

Hornblende-porphyrites occur as dykes in the sandstones around the Distinkhorn granodiorite complex and in the lavas near Knockdon (Dalmellington–Straiton area).

Plagiophyres. The so-called *plagiophyres* form thick sills in the Maybole district, and smaller sills or dykes near Straiton, at Tinto, and in the Pentland Hills. Somewhat similar intrusions occur near Dundee. Plagiophyres may be defined as decomposed sparsely porphyritic or non-porphyritic fine-grained intrusions whose original composition was probably andesitic. The altered feldspars often approximate to oligoclase in composition. Some of the rocks originally contained pyroxene, and others hornblende, as the ferromagnesian constituent.

Microdiorites. Fine-grained sub-basic rocks, perhaps best classed as microdiorites, are fairly numerous, mainly in the form of small dykes, in the Lower Old Red and Silurian areas between Distinkhorn and Tinto.

Kersantites, in the form of sills and dykes, are confined to the Maybole and Straiton districts; they contain abundant fresh biotite and pseudomorphs after pyroxene and olivine.

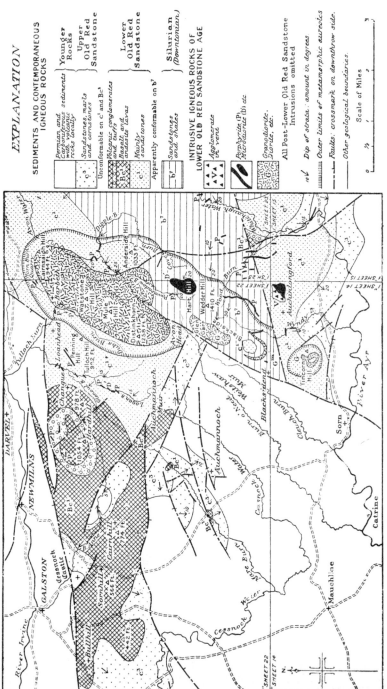

FIG. 6. *Map of Darvel–Galston–Sorn district, Ayrshire and Lanarkshire, showing granodiorite, diorite, etc., of Distinkhorn and Tincorn Hill, and associated minor intrusions and lavas of Lower Old Red Sandstone age*

Pyroxene-porphyrites, including *hypersthene-porphyrites,* occur as dykes, sills, or intrusions of doubtful form, in the vicinity of Dundee, near the Distinkhorn granodiorite complex, at Tincorn Hill, near Dalmellington (*e.g.* north and south of Little Shalloch), Garleffin Fell (Mull of Miljoan) and Maybole (Guiltreehill). Some of these rocks are fine-grained intrusive andesites, while others are transitional to quartz-dolerites.

Quartz-dolerites form a number of intrusions near Dundee, and thick sills south of Maybole and near Garleffin Fell (Black Hill of Knockgardner, Knockin-culloch Hill and Daljedburgh Hill). The Dundee rocks are hypersthene-bearing.

Olivine-dolerites and Basalts. Minor intrusions of olivine-dolerite and basalt of various types have been mapped in Kincardineshire, near Dundee, and in the Maybole and Straiton districts.

Distinkhorn Complex. The most important outcrop of plutonic character is the Distinkhorn Complex, covering 3 square miles of the borders of Ayrshire and Lanarkshire (MacGregor, 1930). The rock-types include *hornblende-biotite-granodiorite,* and older contact-altered *diorite* and *hypersthene-diorite,* and resemble the 'granites' and 'hyperites' of the Southern Uplands. Dykes and sills of Lower Old Red Sandstone age, in the baked sandstones of the aureole surrounding the complex, have been subjected to varying degrees of contact-metamorphism, and provide typical examples of thermally altered minor intrusions (Fig. 6).

Tincorn Hill Complex. Other beautiful examples of contact-altered igneous rocks (notably hypersthene-porphyrites) are found in the smaller *dioritic complex* at Tincorn Hill, a little to the south of Distinkhorn.

Fore Burn Complex. The *dioritic rocks* of the Fore Burn igneous complex, south-east of Straiton, have produced some alteration in adjacent lavas of Lower Old Red Sandstone age. This outcrop is noteworthy because of intense local tourmalinization and the occurrence of iron-sulphide veins. Baked sediments are found around this complex as well as at Tincorn Hill (Plate IV and Fig. 6).

Ochils and Pentlands. Small intrusions of *dioritic rocks* have also been recorded in the Ochil Hills, and in the Pentland Hills (Lyne Water). The intrusions of the Ochils (Duncrevie, Tillicoultry) carry enstatite or hypersthene.

MAIN OUTCROPS AND SELECTED REFERENCES (IGNEOUS ROCKS)
General.

1897. GEIKIE, Sir A., *The Ancient Volcanoes of Great Britain,* vol. i, pp. 263–311.
1901. HEDDLE, M. F., *The Mineralogy of Scotland,* vol. i (Douglas, Edinburgh), pp. 55–84 (Agates, etc.).

1931. Guppy, E. M., and H. H. Thomas, Chemical Analyses of Igneous Rocks, Metamorphic Rocks and Minerals (*Mem. Geol. Surv.*) pp. 15, 17, 19, 23, 24, 34, 36, 39, 48, 49, 64, 68.

Near Highland Boundary Fault.

1928. Allan, D. A., The Geology of the Highland Border from Tayside to Noranside, *Trans. Roy. Soc. Edin.*, vol. lvi, part i, pp. 57–88.
1940. Allan, D. A., The Geology of the Highland Border from Glen Almond to Glen Artney, *Trans. Roy. Soc. Edin.*, vol. lx, part i, pp. 171–193.
1947. Anderson, J. G. C., The Geology of the Highland Border: Stonehaven to Arran, *Trans. Roy. Soc. Edin.*, vol. xi, part ii, pp. 479–515.

Kincardineshire: north of Montrose.

1913. Campbell, R., The Geology of South-Eastern Kincardineshire, *Trans. Roy. Soc. Edin.*, vol., xlviii, part iv, pp. 923–960.

Forfarshire (Angus): south-west of Montrose.

1913. Jowett, A., The Volcanic Rocks of the Forfarshire Coast and the associated Sediments, *Quart. Journ. Geol. Soc.*, vol. lxix, pp. 459–482.

Sidlaw Hills District: Arbroath to Perth.

1928. Harris, J. W., The Intrusive Igneous Rocks of the Dundee District, *Trans. Edin. Geol. Soc.*, vol. xii, part i, pp. 53–68.
1928. Harris, J. W., Notes on the Extrusive Rocks of the Dundee District, *ibid.*, pp. 105–110.
1932. Davidson, C. F., The Geology of Moncrieffe Hill, Perthshire, *Geol. Mag.*, pp. 452–464.
1934. Balsillie, D., Petrography of the Intrusive Igneous Rocks of South Angus, *Trans. amd Proc. Perthshire Soc. Nat. Sci.*, vol. ix, part iv, pp. 133–145.

Ochil Hills District: Tayport to Bridge of Allan.

1897. Flett, J. S., A Hypersthene-andesite from Dumyat (Ochils), *Trans. Edin. Geol. Soc.*, vol. vii, part iii, pp. 290–297.
1900. Geikie, A., and H. Kynaston, in The Geology of Central and Western Fife and Kinross-shire (*Mem. Geol. Surv.*), pp. 15–32 and 252–260.
1902. Geikie, A., and J. S. Flett, in The Geology of Eastern Fife (*Mem. Geol. Surv.*), pp. 33–54 and 386–388.
1927. Read, H. H., The Western Ochil Hills, *Proc. Geol. Assoc.*, vol. xxxviii, pp. 492–494.
1939. Walker, F., A Quartz-diorite from Glenduckie Hill, Fife, *Geol. Mag.*, pp. 72–76.

Pentland Hills District.

1910. Peach, B. N., and J. S. Flett, in The Geology of the Neighbourhood of Edinburgh (*Mem. Geol. Surv.*), pp. 19–41.

Biggar–Tinto District: West Linton to New Cumnock.

1925. Read, H. H., and J. Phemister, in Summary of Progress for 1924 (*Mem. Geol. Surv.*), pp. 99–103.
1926. Read, H. H., in Summary of Progress for 1925 (*Mem. Geol. Surv.*), pp. 105–107.
1927. Read, H. H., The Tinto District, *Proc. Geol. Assoc.*, vol. xxxviii, pp. 499–504.

Dalmellington-Straiton and Maybole Districts: Ayrshire.
Maybole, or Brown Carrick Hill District: south-west of Ayr.
1910. SMITH, John, Semi-Precious Stones of Carrick (Cross, Kilwinning), 82 pp.
1914. TYRRELL, G. W., A Petrographical Sketch of the Carrick Hills, Ayrshire, *Trans. Geol. Soc. Glasgow*, vol. xv, part i, pp. 64–83.
1929. EYLES, V. A., J. B. SIMPSON and A. G. MACGREGOR, The Igneous Geology of Central Ayrshire, *Trans. Geol. Soc. Glasgow*, vol. xviii, part iii, pp. 363–369.
1949. EYLES, V. A., and A. G. MACGREGOR, in The Geology of Central Ayrshire (*Mem. Geol. Surv.*), Chapter III.

Distinkhorn–Tincorn Hill District: on Ayrshire–Lanarkshire border.
1930. MACGREGOR, A. G., in The Geology of North Ayrshire (*Mem. Geol. Surv.*), pp. 19–55.

Muirkirk–Lesmahagow District.
There is no literature dealing with the numerous felsitic sills of this area. Lavas do not occur.

2. UPPER OLD RED SANDSTONE

The deposition of the Upper Old Red Sandstone was preceded by a period of folding and denudation. Its members rest unconformably on older rocks, on different horizons within the Lower Old Red Sandstone succession, on Silurian strata, or even on the crystalline schists of the Highlands. On the other hand it passes conformably upwards into the Carboniferous, and was at one time regarded as part of the Calciferous Sandstone Series.

Rocks of this age occur on the north side of the Campsie and Kilpatrick Hills, where, near Killearn, they attain 2,700 ft. in thickness.

The Upper Old Red reappears farther east in the Howe of Fife (Kinross plain and Strath Eden) where the succession, consisting of sandstones, marls and conglomerates generally of a brick-red colour, is estimated to be about 1,500 ft. thick. Near the eastern end of this outcrop ($2\frac{1}{4}$ miles east of Cupar) occurs the famous fish-locality of Dura Den on the banks of the Ceres Burn. To the north of the Ochil Hills, again, Upper Old Red Sandstone strata underlie part of the Carse of Gowrie along the Firth of Tay, while outliers of the same Series appear on the Forfar–Kincardine coast in the neighbourhood of Arbroath and St. Cyrus.

Along the south-eastern side of the Midland Valley Upper Old Red Sandstone strata occur at a number of localities between Dunbar and New Cumnock (Plate VIII). In south-central Ayrshire, again, they are found along a semi-circular belt extending from the coast south of the Heads of Ayr to near Straiton.

Farther north the Upper Old Red Sandstone appears in several outcrops on the south side of the Irvine valley where its thickness is well over 500 ft., and covers a considerable area along the Firth of Clyde from Ardrossan (thickness over 1,000 ft.) northwards past Fairlie and Largs to Wemyss Bay. Red sandstones of this age are present also in Bute and the Great Cumbrae.

Contemporaneous igneous rocks are practically unknown in the Upper Old Red of the Midland Valley but at the base of the Carboniferous lavas of the

Campsie Fells, north of Kilsyth, a few flows of basalt are intercalated in strata assigned to this formation.

Types of Sediment. The main types of sediment are:

Sandstones. These form by far the greater part of the succession. They are typically bright red in colour, often false-bedded and frequently pebbly. In their generally brighter hues and more quartzose character they contrast with those of the Lower Old Red which are more sombre and much more feldspathic and micaceous. In the upper part of the Series, however, light yellow and whitish sandstones occur, and these paler colours are characteristic of the Upper Old Red of Central Ayrshire.

The red sandstones have supplied locally considerable quantities of valuable building stone: *e.g.* Craigmillar Quarries, near Edinburgh; quarries in the Wemyss Bay district and near Dunbar, etc. From sandstones of this age in the neighbourhood of Edinburgh large supplies of excellent water have been obtained for brewing and other purposes.

Marls and Marly Shales. These are soft, chocolate-red, purplish or sometimes greenish and mottled deposits, varying from poorly-bedded and somewhat calcareous mudstones to micaceous and sandy shales. They are quite subordinate to the sandstones.

Conglomerates. Conglomerates and pebbly grits are locally common at the base of the Series (*e.g.* near Arbroath) and bands of conglomerate are also met with at higher horizons.

Cornstones. Concretions of impure and sandy limestone (cornstone) are a characteristic feature of the Upper Old Red Sandstone. In most districts they become more abundant in the higher part of the sequence and frequently occur aggregated into nodular layers or solid bands which have in the past been extensively quarried or mined for agricultural purposes. Locally cornstone may occur at the base of the Series.

Conditions of Deposition. The Upper Old Red Sandstone sediments appear to have been deposited over a slowly-subsiding area subjected to periodic flooding and desiccation. The local basal conglomerates represent the products of torrential stream-erosion but as subsidence and deposition went on this early phase gave place to one of shallow continental basins. The deposits that accumulated in these basins were partly fluviatile and partly lacustrine. The evidence for contemporaneous erosion at many horizons, the occurrence of desiccation-breccias and the presence of sun-cracked surfaces, point to alternations of humid and arid conditions. Wind-rounded grains of quartz, though in no way characteristic of the formation, have been recorded at several localities and, in conjunction with the occasional presence of dreikanter, show that at times desert conditions locally prevailed. The cornstones possibly represent a subsoil replacement deposit similar in origin to the kankar of tropical regions of the present day (*see* 'Glasgow District Memoir').

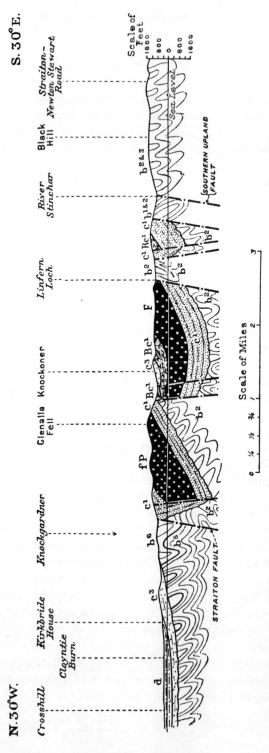

Fig. 7. Section across Silurian and Ordovician inliers, at Knockgardner and Linfern Loch, near Straiton, Ayrshire, showing unconformities below Lower and Upper Old Red Sandstone and folding and faulting of Lower Old Red igneous rocks

b^1, b^2 and b^3 = Ordovician; b^5 and b^6 = Silurian; Lower Old Red Sandstone: c^1 = sandstone and conglomerate, Bc^1 = basalt lava, F = felsite sill, fP = acid porphyrite sill; c^3 = Upper Old Red Sandstone; d = Carboniferous

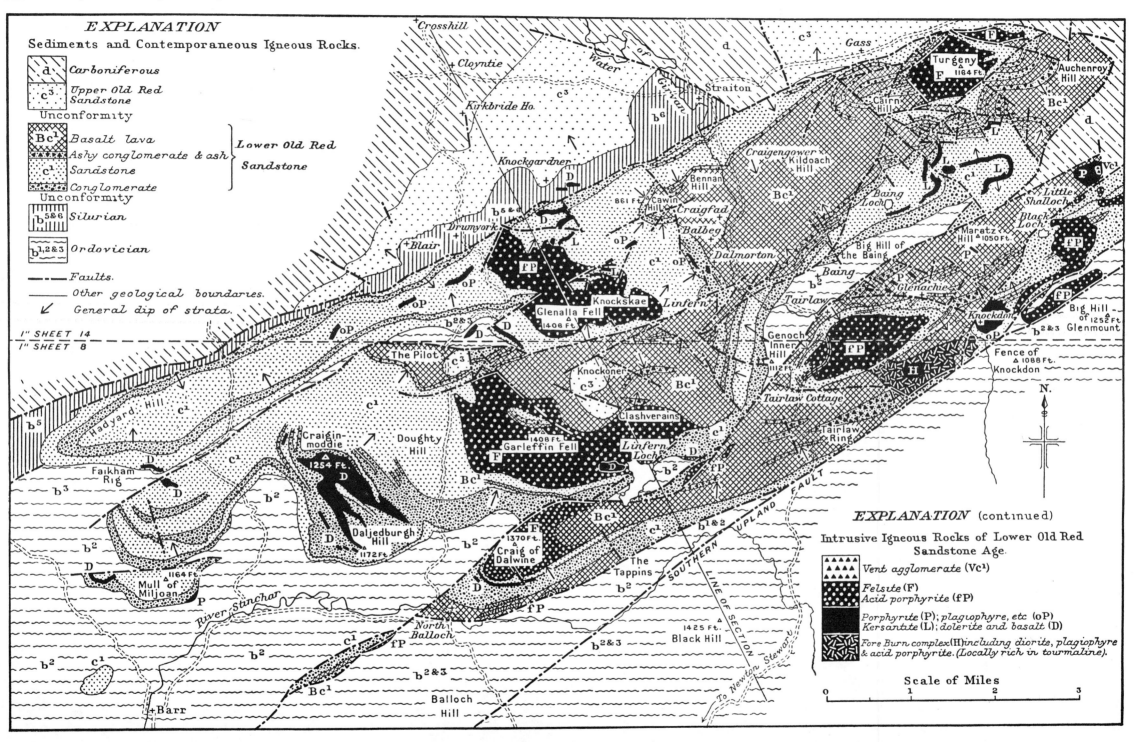

(For explanation, *see* p. vii.)

MAP OF THE DISTRICT NEAR BARR AND STRAITON, AYRSHIRE

The Upper Old Red Sandstone passes up conformably into the Carboniferous. Passage-beds between the two formations have been described from a number of localities; in many areas it is difficult to decide where the dividing line should be drawn (see Glasgow District and North Ayrshire Memoirs; also Tait, 1939; Macgregor and others, 1940). Interbanding of strata characteristic of the Upper Old Red Sandstone with strata typical of the Cementstone Group—e.g. of the cornstone facies with the Ballagan facies—has been recorded (Kennedy and MacGregor, 1930; Richey, 1949).

PALAEONTOLOGY

Fish-remains have been obtained from a number of localities within the Midland Valley but rarely occur in abundance. The most prolific locality is that of Dura Den near Cupar, Fife, which yielded the following forms:—*Bothriolepis hydrophila, Phyllolepis concentrica, Glyptopomus minor, G. kinnairdi, Gyroptychius heddlei, Holoptychius flemingi, Phaneropleuron andersoni.* By far the commonest form is *Holoptychius flemingi.*

Phyllolepis concentrica has also been recorded from Clashbennie in the Carse of Gowrie; *Holoptychius nobilissimus* has been obtained from Clashbennie, from below Salisbury Craigs, Edinburgh, from near Whittinghame, East Lothian, and from various localities in Fife; *Bothriolepis major* has been found at Bracken Bay near the Heads of Ayr.

SELECTED REFERENCES

1908. HICKLING, G., The Old Red Sandstone of Forfarshire, *Geol. Mag.*, pp. 403–407.
1912. CRAIG, R. M., and D. BALSILLIE, The Geology of the Country around Dundee, *Brit. Assoc. Handbook*, Dundee, pp. 545–547, 551–553.
1913. CAMPBELL, R., The Geology of South-Eastern Kincardineshire, *Trans. Roy. Soc. Edin.*, vol. xlviii, part iv, pp. 955–956.
1915. HORNE, J., A. S. WOODWARD and others, The Upper Old Red Sandstone of Dura Den, *Report Brit. Assoc.*, Australia, 1914, pp. 116–123.
1930. KENNEDY, W. Q., and A. G. MACGREGOR, in Summary of Progress for 1929, Part I (*Mem. Geol. Surv.*), pp. 72, 73.
1939. TAIT, D., Recent Bores for Water in Edinburgh and the Correlation of some Bore Sections, *Trans. Edin. Geol. Soc.*, vol. xiii, part iv, pp. 445–452.
1940. MACGREGOR, M., and others, Discussion on the Boundary between the Old Red Sandstone and the Carboniferous, The Advancement of Science, vol. i, No. 2 (*Rep. Brit. Assoc.*), pp. 256–258.
1942. MACGREGOR, M., The Leven Valley, Dumbartonshire, *Trans. Geol. Soc. Glasgow*, vol. xx, part ii, p. 124.
1949. RICHEY, J. E., in The Geology of Central Ayrshire (*Mem. Geol. Surv*), Chapter V (Upper Old Red Facies in Cementstone Group).
See also Geological Survey Memoirs (p. 94) on Fife, East Lothian, Neighbourhood of Edinburgh, Glasgow District, North Ayrshire, and Central Ayrshire.

V. CARBONIFEROUS

ROCKS of this age occupy much the greater part of the Midland Valley. The subdivisions and principal index-horizons are shown, together with other information, in Fig. 8 (p. 35). These subdivisions represent an essentially litho-logical classification and brief descriptions of each of them will now be given.

Calciferous Sandstone Series. This series is subdivided into a Lower or Cementstone Group consisting mainly of rapidly alternating shales and thin bands of argillaceous dolomite known as cementstones, and an Upper Group, usually much thicker, which in the Lothians and parts of Fife contains workable oil-shales (p. 40) and is for this reason often referred to as the Oil-Shale Group. Over large areas this Upper Group is largely, sometimes almost entirely, replaced by contemporaneous igneous rocks (Figs. 8 and 11).

Lower Limestone Group. This group consists mainly of shales (blaes) and limestones, although a certain proportion of sandy beds is usually present in addition. The shales often carry numerous clayband ironstone nodules or ribs. Certain of the limestones locally attain a thickness of as much as 60 ft. but they are as a rule thin. A few coals are also present though seldom of workable thickness.

Limestone Coal Group (*Edge Coal Group of Midlothian*). This group consists of alternating sandstones, shaly sandstones and shales, with subordinate coals, fireclays and ironstones. The coals are widely wrought. The clayband and black-band ironstones were at one time of great importance in the industrial life of Scotland (p. 40) and still yield small supplies of ore. In the upper part of the group sandstones predominate, in the lower part shales.

Upper Limestone Group. This group is essentially arenaceous in character but contains a number of thick beds of shale, four to eight limestones and a few, generally thin, coals. The individual limestones rarely exceed 10 ft.

The limestones in the Lower and Upper Limestone Groups are all marine and along with the shales associated with them have yielded a rich and abundant fauna.

Millstone Grit. This series consists mainly of sandstone, sometimes coarse-grained and pebbly, with shales, fireclays, 'ganisters' and a few impersistent, generally thin, coals. It is the source of most of the valuable refractory fireclays and 'ganisters'. Over much of North Ayrshire (as well as in Arran and Kintyre) it is represented, largely or wholly, by contemporaneous igneous rocks (Fig. 11).

Productive Coal Measures. This group is built up of white and yellowish sandstones, sandy shales, dark-blue or black shales, and fireclays, intercalated in which are a number of important coal seams. Ironstones, both blackband and clayband, are also present but nowadays are not of much importance.

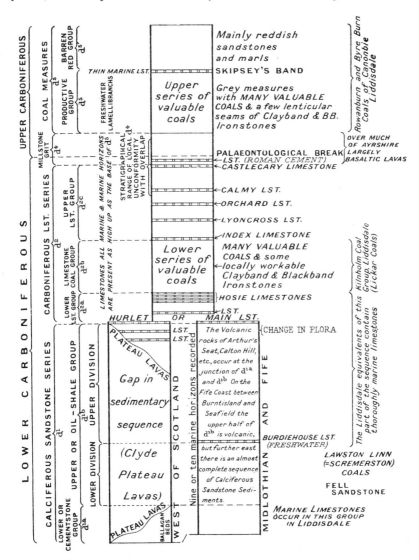

FIG. 8. *Diagram showing general succession in the Carboniferous of the Midland Valley of Scotland, with subdivisions and principal index horizons, and probable equivalents south of the Silurian Tableland*

Barren Red Coal Measures. This group consists essentially of massive, usually soft and reddish, sandstones, with variegated marly fireclays, purplish shales, occasional thin coals, and a few ribs of impure limestone sometimes containing *Spirorbis.*

VARIATION IN THICKNESS OF CARBONIFEROUS SEDIMENTS

	AYRSHIRE, NORTH	CENTRAL COALFIELD[1]			FIFE	
		GLASGOW	KILSYTH	N.E. STIRLING-SHIRE	W.	E.
	Ft.	Ft.	Ft.	Ft.	Ft.	Ft.
BARREN RED COAL MEASURES	300+	960+	—	—	—	1,000+
PRODUCTIVE COAL MEASURES	700	c. 1,000 (Uddingston–Bothwell)	—	—	—	c. 1,700
MILLSTONE GRIT	530[2]	c. 320	—	1,125	1,060	—
UPPER LIMESTONE GROUP	261	c. 900 (Springburn–Glenboig)	1,360	1,638	1,530	—
LIMESTONE COAL GROUP	650	1,110	1,320	945	1,620	—
LOWER LIMESTONE GROUP	120	480	700	384	610	—
CALCIFEROUS SST. SERIES { UPPER GROUP (with oil-shales locally)	Thin; Volcanic Group	Up to 1,080; Volcanic Group	—	—	—	c. 3,800
CEMENTSTONE GROUP }	—	700+	—	—	—	?500

(1) The Central Coalfield includes the whole of One-inch Sheet 31, the eastern part of Sheet 30, the northern part of Sheet 23, and small portions of Sheets 22, 24, 32 and 39

(2) Volcanic rocks

Variation in Thickness of Sediments. The Carboniferous sediments attain their greatest thickness in Fife. The table opposite illustrates the marked diminution encountered as they are followed south-westwards into North Ayrshire, the figures indicating, approximately, the maximum thicknesses in the different districts.

Marked variations also occur within each of the main coalfields. In parts of Ayrshire, for example, the Carboniferous Limestone Series is reduced to less than 100 ft. These variations are in the main due to actual attenuation of the sediments and not to non-deposition or overlap. They are brought about by the thickening or thinning of every part of the succession and indicate the operation of differential crustal movements over the area of deposition. In some cases the variations take place abruptly across north-easterly lines now closely followed by lines of later faulting (*e.g.* the Dusk Water and Inchgotrick faults in North Ayrshire and the Kerse Loch fault in Central Ayrshire; see 'Geology of North Ayrshire' and 'Economic Geology of the Ayrshire Coalfields, Area IV,' both *Mems. Geol. Surv.*). It seems certain that movements along these lines must have been in progress during the deposition of the sediments.

The maximum known thickness for the Barren Red Coal Measures is 1,776 ft.; this figure is obtained from Central Ayrshire where the Carboniferous is overlain by Permian lavas. There is probably an unconformity at the base of the lavas, however, and part of the Barren Measures may be absent.

Types of Sediment. The sedimentary succession outlined above is built up mainly of sandstones, shales (*i.e.* blaes or mudstones), and rock-types intermediate between these, *i.e.* shaly sandstones (fakes) and sandy shales (faky blaes). Subordinate to these are the limestones, coals, ironstones, oil-shales, fireclays and marls.

Sandstones. The principal sandstone horizons occur in the Oil-Shale Group, Upper Limestone Group, Millstone Grit and Coal Measures. Those in the first two groups are light-coloured and as a rule fine-textured, and some of them have been extensively quarried and mined for building stone. The Millstone Grit, although dominantly arenaceous, does not yield good freestone; it is composed mainly of somewhat massive, often current-bedded sandstones varying much in texture and colour. Characteristic features of the series in Midlothian and Fife are the dominantly red tints and the abundance of pebbly layers. The sandstones of the Productive Coal Measures are grey or yellowish, in marked contrast to those of the overlying Barren Group which are, as a rule, reddish and coarse in texture. Both groups have furnished important supplies of building stone.

Some of the argillaceous sandstones ('ganisters') associated with the refractory fireclays of the Millstone Grit are mined along with these and used in the manufacture of refractory goods. The more siliceous varieties are also used locally for this purpose or for the manufacture of bottle-glass. Certain sandstones in the Upper Limestone Group are crushed for moulding sand.

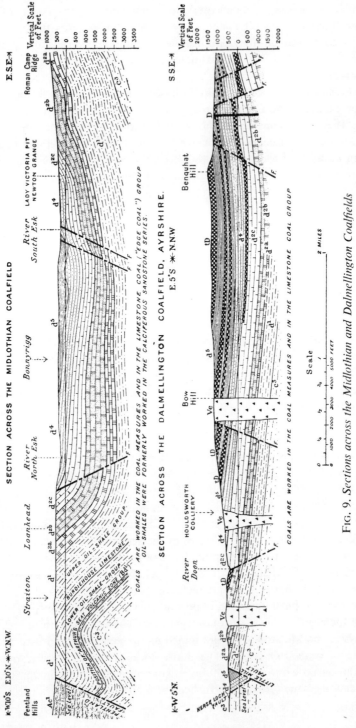

FIG. 9. *Sections across the Midlothian and Dalmellington Coalfields*

Ac^1 = Lower Old Red Sandstone lava; c^3 = Upper Old Red Sandstone; Carboniferous: d^1 = Calciferous Sandstone Series, d^{2a} = Lower Limestone Group, d^{2b} = Limestone Coal Group, d^{2c} = Upper Limestone Group, d^4 = Millstone Grit, d^5 = Productive Coal Measures; tD = teschenitic sill; D = basic dyke; Ve = Permian neck; F = fault

Shales (mudstones) are widely distributed throughout the succession but are specially characteristic of the Cementstone Group, upper part of the Oil-Shale Group, Lower Limestone Group, and lower part of the Limestone Coal Group. Bands of this material are used locally in the manufacture of bricks. Where baked by igneous intrusions they may form valuable honestones (Water of Ayr Stone). Alum shale was at one time worked in the Glasgow district.

Limestones. Marine limestones are found mainly in the upper part of the Calciferous Sandstone Series, and in the Lower and Upper Limestone Groups. Those in the two last-named subdivisions are widespread and persistent horizons. Long wrought at their outcrops for agricultural purposes, the thicker seams have also been quarried and mined locally for use as a flux in blast-furnaces, for cement manufacture, etc. Marine horizons are present in the Limestone Coal Group. Millstone Grit and Coal Measures but definite limestones are rare and thin.

Freshwater limestones occur on certain horizons. The best known is the Burdiehouse Limestone in the Oil-Shale Group, locally as much as 50 ft. in thickness. In the volcanic areas limestones referred to the action of hot springs supplying shallow pools are occasionally met with, *e.g.* the East Kirkton Limestone of the Bathgate Hills and the Pettycur Limestone of the Burntisland coast.

Coals. The chief repositories of valuable coals are the Limestone Coal Group and the Productive Coal Measures. Coals also occur in the other subdivisions of the Carboniferous, but are seldom of much economic importance.

The principal varieties of coal represented are listed below:

(*a*) *Bituminous Coals*, in which the volatile matter varies from about 30 to 40 per cent, are by far the most abundant and are extensively wrought for household use and for various industrial purposes. They include the *coking* and the so-called *splint* coals. The former are characterized by their bright lustre and by their property of fusing at about 1,000° C. to form a dense hard coke suitable for metallurgical work. The splint coals are hard and dull in appearance and do not cake or break up readily when heated; formerly widely sought after for use in blast-furnaces, they are still in demand for steam-raising in locomotive boilers, etc.

(*b*) *Cannel* (*i.e.* Candle) or *Gas Coals*, in which the volatile matter exceeds 40 per cent, were at one time extensively employed in the manufacture of illuminating gas and were also worked locally as a source of oil. They are still used to a limited extent for enriching coal-gas. The cannels occur generally as lenticular bands in association with the bituminous coals.

(*c*) *Steam Coals*, in which the volatile matter averages 15 to 25 per cent, are used for steam-raising where smokeless combustion is desired.

(*d*) *Anthracites*, in which the volatile matter is usually below 10 per cent, are employed mainly in central heating installations requiring slow smokeless combustion. They are also used in malting. The anthracites are confined to certain limited areas in which they are nearly always associated with sheets of igneous rock (sills) intruded a short distance above or below the seam.[1]

The earliest records of coal-mining in Scotland refer to outcrop workings of the Smithy Coal at Bo'ness in the latter part of the twelfth century. Workings of this kind were followed by shallow pits drained at first by adits and later by a simple chain-and-bucket system of pumping. The introduction of the steam-engine to pump water and wind coal led to the development of the coalfields on an intensive scale. The first Newcomen atmospheric steam-engine was erected about 1720 at Elphinstone Colliery in Stirlingshire and it was in 1769 that James Watt built at Bo'ness his first steam-engine for raising coal.

Ironstones. Clayband ironstones, composed of soluble ferrous carbonate (with some manganese and magnesium) and an insoluble clay basis, are widely distributed in the Carboniferous rocks. They occur as balls, nodules or ribs in the various beds of shale. It was from surface or shallow workings in nodules or ribs of this kind that the early ironworks of the Midland Valley drew their supplies.

Claybands which contain sufficient carbonaceous matter to render them self-calcining are known as blackband ironstones. They are all impersistent lenticular deposits, rarely exceeding 12 or 14 in. in thickness and are often associated in composite seams with gas or cannel coal.

It was at Carron Ironworks, founded in 1759, that Carboniferous claybands were first used and smelted with coal to produce pig-iron. Prior to that date it was made from imported ore at a few localities in the West Highlands where wood-charcoal could easily be obtained. Blackband was discovered near Airdrie in 1801, but it was not until the perfection of the Neilson hot-blast process in 1828 that such ores began to be used. The production of ironstone in Scotland reached its maximum during the period 1874–1884, the greatest yield being 2,660,000 tons in 1880, but by 1913 had fallen to 600,000 tons. Among the factors contributing to this decline must be noted the exhaustion of the richer and most accessible fields and the increasing costs of working the thinner and lower-grade seams. At the present time very little ironstone is mined in Scotland.

Oil-Shales. The valuable oil-shales of Scotland are found in the Upper Calciferous Sandstone rocks (Oil-Shale Group) as developed in West Lothian, Midlothian and parts of Fife. Typical Lothian oil-shale is a fine-grained, tough, and sometimes flexible material, with a dark-brown or black colour. It is minutely laminated, yields a brown streak, and when cut with a sharp knife gives thin shavings which readily curl. On distillation in retorts in the absence of air and in presence of steam the organic matter undergoes decomposition, with the production of what is called "crude oil" and of ammonia derived from a portion of the nitrogen of the shale. The crude oil is subjected to fractional distillation

[1] For Graphite, see p. 83.

to produce the various burning, lubricating and cleaning oils marketed, while the ammonia is converted into ammonium sulphate.

It was in 1851 that James Young established at Bathgate a plant to produce oil by distillation from the once famous Boghead Coal or Torbanite Mineral, a very rich type of cannel coal found in this neighbourhood over a very limited area. The supplies of the material were soon exhausted but in 1858 oil-shale was discovered near Broxburn and the industry thereafter centred in West Lothian. Improved methods of manufacture and concentration upon the production of lubricating oils, paraffin wax and sulphate of ammonia enabled it to withstand the competition of imported petroleum products. The output of shale reached a maximum of approximately $3\frac{1}{4}$ million tons in 1913, but between the wars economic difficulties led to a restriction of operations and in 1933 the output had fallen to a little less than $1\frac{1}{2}$ million tons. Nowadays attention is concentrated upon the production of motor spirit, solvent naphthas, burning oils and paraffin wax.

Fireclays. The Millstone Grit supplies most of the refractory fireclays and 'ganisters' found in Scotland. The coal 'underseats' in both the Limestone Coal Group and Productive Coal Measures are also important sources of fireclay for the production of bricks, sanitary ware or refractory goods. The Ayrshire Bauxitic Clay overlying the Millstone Grit lavas of North Ayrshire (p. 34) and produced by their contemporaneous weathering and decomposition, has attracted attention in recent years; it has been used in the manufacture of alum and for special kinds of refractory ware.

'Marls.' The deposits included under this name are well developed in the Oil-Shale Group of the Lothians and in the sediments which, in the west of Scotland, succeed the Calciferous Sandstone volcanic rocks. They consist of fine-grained argillaceous sediments in massive beds separated by ribs of hard sandstone; carbonates in the form of scattered particles or aggregates of small grains are sometimes present. 'Marly' beds, with little or no calcareous content, occur in the Barren Red Coal Measures.

Conditions of Deposition. The Cementstone Group of the Midland Valley, with its characteristic rhythmical alternation of shales and thin ribs of argillaceous dolomite of chemical origin, and its sun-cracked and ripple-marked surfaces (Ballagan facies; cf. p. 33), appears to have been deposited in inland sheets of water subjected to periodic desiccation. Organic remains are rare, consisting for the most part of plant and fish-remains and a few small crustaceans (*Estheria*). Only occasionally have freshwater mussels (*Anthraconauta minima*) or *Lingula* (*L. mytiloides*) been recorded.

The Oil-Shale Group of the Lothians is characterized by a special type of sedimentation developed over a restricted area (p. 40) bordered by land masses of older rocks. Alternating lagoonal and estuarine conditions prevailed through-out the deposition of the greater part of the sediments. "The whole group is

D

clearly of shallow-water origin, and was deposited over an area marked by intermittent subsidence of irregular amount, where incursions of the open sea were extremely rare. Much of the sediments must have accumulated under mud-flat conditions, for sun-cracks and 'desiccation-breccias' are commonly met with especially in the marly strata that bulk so largely in the series" (Carruthers, 1927, pp. 3–4). The oil-shales represent fine-grained inorganic material impregnated with carbonaceous substance derived partly from plant, partly from animal, remains. In East Fife, where rocks of the same age are well-developed, they consist of a rapidly alternating series of sandstones, shales, thin coals and fire-clays with thin limestones and shelly bands; marine fossils occur on ten separate horizons, indicating periodic incursions of the sea.

As shown by the diagram on p. 35, volcanic activity on an extensive scale broke out early in Carboniferous times and a great part of the Calciferous Sandstone succession is locally composed of volcanic rocks (mainly lavas). In these areas there is a threefold subdivision into:—Upper Sedimentary Group, Volcanic Group, Lower Sedimentary (or Cementstone) Group. The lavas of this period, poured out subaerially from pipe-like vents which were sometimes aligned as if following a line of crustal weakness, built up great volcanic platforms (Clyde Plateau, Garleton Hills, etc.) in places 2,000 to 3,000 ft. thick. Individual flows frequently show the rotted upper surfaces, and the development of 'bole,' characteristic of lavas subjected to contemporaneous weathering. Although locally some flows were erupted on the margins of lagoons, and were soon covered by water (e.g. Arthur's Seat and Bathgate Hills), not a single example of a true pillow-lava has been found. There is clear evidence that the lavas were subjected at the close of the volcanic episode to prolonged subaerial denudation. The strata of the Upper Sedimentary Group rest upon them with marked unconformity and the first sediments to be laid down were derived directly from the weathering of the lavas (basal volcanic detritus).

The close of Calciferous Sandstone times was marked by a widespread submergence which carried nearly the whole region beneath the Carboniferous Limestone sea. The Hurlet Limestone (Fig. 8) ushers in a new epoch when the lagoons and land-barriers of the older period were alike submerged. The Carboniferous Limestone Series is characterized throughout by a well-marked sedimentary rhythm, indicating successive stages in the general movement of depression. Sedimentary cycles recur again and again throughout the succession, indicating (1) the subsidence of a land-area below the waters of a shallow sea, (2) the formation of a marine limestone, (3) the subsequent shoaling of the sea by the accumulation of detrital matter, and (4) the formation of a fresh land-surface. Frequently, however, the cycle is broken or incomplete and, in the Limestone Coal Group for example, the periodic movements of subsidence were rarely sufficient to allow of the establishment of marine conditions.

Volcanic activity manifested itself in a number of areas in Carboniferous Limestone times (Fig. 11) especially in the form of numerous vents of explosive type.

Marked physiographic changes again supervened at the end of Carboniferous Limestone times. There was a general uplift of the whole region, accompanied by increased denudation of the land-areas to the north or north-east. The false-bedded Millstone Grit sandstones with their irregular pebbly layers represent material laid down in deltas of large rivers. The interbedded shales, on the other hand, were accumulated in quiet water during periods of relatively greater subsidence, sometimes under estuarine, sometimes under marine, conditions.

There is a marked contrast between the arenaceous deposits of the Millstone Grit and the fine-grained, dark-coloured mudstones in the lower part of the Productive Coal Measures. Here the recurring cycles of sedimentation rarely show evidence of marine conditions. The numerous fireclays and coals represent old land-surfaces; the vegetation that gave rise to the coals grew in swamps and was preserved from destruction by the fact that it accumulated in a water-logged condition. The dark shales which overlie many of the coals indicate a slight periodic subsidence which allowed muddy detritus to accumulate. During flood-periods sandy materials were deposited and gradually a fresh land-surface formed. The characteristic fossils of the Productive Coal Measures are the freshwater lamellibranchs ('mussels'; see pp. 46–49). Estuarine fish are also present and occasionally the remains of amphibia (*Anthracosaurus* and *Loxomma*).

The Barren Red Coal Measures, with their variegated mudstones and marly beds, their sun-cracked surfaces and numerous 'desiccation-breccias' must have originated largely under semi-arid conditions. Coal seams, usually thin, are some-times present, especially in the lower part of the group. Fossils are few, although at certain horizons freshwater ostracoda (*Carbonita*) and 'mussels' have been obtained. Varied coloration is characteristic of this group and the red staining of the sandstones is probably secondary.

PALAEONTOLOGY

Palaeontological research has shown that the Carboniferous sediments fall into two series, Lower and Upper Carboniferous. The former includes the Calciferous Sandstone Series, the Carboniferous Limestone Series and the lower part of the Millstone Grit; the Upper Carboniferous comprises the upper two-thirds of the Millstone Grit and the Coal Measures.

Upper and Lower Carboniferous. Kidston and Traquair, working on the fossil plants and fishes respectively, demonstrated that a marked palaeontological 'break' occurred in the lower part of the Millstone Grit. The plants obtained from the Carboniferous rocks *above* the 'break' are, with a few exceptions, specifically distinct from those found *below* it. In the case of the estuarine fishes, again, nearly all the Lower Carboniferous species, and with them also a number of genera, are replaced above the 'break' by a new assemblage.

The data furnished by the invertebrate fauna are not so conclusive, but the evidence of the gastropods and marine lamellibranchs points to a marked faunal change soon after the close of Upper Limestone Group times. A number of species (e.g. *Prothyris elegans* Meek), obtained from the lower part of the Millstone Grit, were regarded by Wheelton Hind as identical with forms found in the Coal Measures of Nebraska and Illinois ('Nebraskan Fauna'); many of these, again, have been recorded from Russia, in late-Carboniferous rocks. The brachiopods found at certain horizons in the lower part of the Millstone Grit appear to have Upper Carboniferous affinities or at least to suggest a post-Visean age, e.g. *Productus* (*Productus*) *carbonarius* de Kon., *Productus* (*Linoproductus*) cf. *cora* d'Orb., and *Meekella leei*, although in the case of this group the faunal modification had begun at a somewhat earlier date. *Meekella*, for example, is recorded from the Upper Limestones of North Ayrshire. The giganteid *Producti*, again, do not extend, so far as is known, into the highest beds of the Carboniferous Limestone Series and accordingly the dividing line would, in this case, be drawn some little distance below the Castlecary Limestone. The difference in the stratigraphical position of the 'break' is not, however, great.

The evidence of the goniatites and of the non-marine lamellibranchs also adds support to the view that a 'break' of considerable magnitude occurs within the Millstone Grit.

The significance of the palaeontological 'break' is a question of considerable difficulty. It seems clear, however, that it must be correlated with the evidence obtained within recent years for unconformity within the Millstone Grit. In a number of districts the Lower Carboniferous rocks were uplifted in early Millstone Grit times and subjected to denudation. Along the south side of the Central Coalfield nearly the whole of the Millstone Grit as well as part of the Upper Limestone Group is locally absent through erosion accompanied by overlap. The absence of the Castlecary Limestone over large tracts of this coalfield and in North Ayrshire is ascribed to erosion in early Millstone Grit times. In parts of South Lanarkshire, again, strata referred to the Millstone Grit overlap upon Lower Limestones, and in West-Central Ayrshire Millstone Grit lavas rest locally upon Upper Calciferous Sandstone sediments or even overlie almost directly strata of Cementstone Group age.

CARBONIFEROUS FLORAS

RADSTOCKIAN (Only Keele Group represented in Scotland). =UPPER COAL MEASURES. The Cyatheites-Pecopterids (e.g. *Asterotheca arborescens* (Schl.) and *Acitheca polymorpha* Brongt.) are distinctive. *Calamites* and *Lepidodendron* infrequent.

STAFFORDIAN =TRANSITION SERIES. Flora transitional.

YORKIAN

Sigillaria very abundant.
Lepidodendron abundant.
Calamites common.
Characteristic species include *Asterotheca miltoni* (Artis), *Dactylotheca plumosa* (Artis); and examples of the genera *Odontopteris, Linopteris, Neuropteris, Lonchopteris, Alethopteris* and *Mariopteris*. Many typical *Sphenopterids*.
The dividing line is now drawn in the Central Coalfield at the Ell Coal.

PRE-YORKIAN

Sigillaria not common.
Lepidodendron fairly common (especially *L. aculeatum* Sternb., and *L. obovatum* Sternb.).
Calamites suckowi Brongt. and *C. undulatus* Sternb. common; most other species of *Calamites* rare.
Common forms are:—*Mariopteris nervosa* (Brongt.), *Neuropteris heterophylla* Brongt., *N.gigantea* Sternb.,*Renaultia gracilis* (Brongt.). Rarer species occur, some of which are restricted to the Pre-Yorkian.
With one or two exceptions the Floras above and below this line are specifically distinct.

(Upper Carboniferous — left margin divisions:)
Part of Barren Red Measures (only in Liddisdale and Ayrshire)
Upper part of Productive Coal Measures and lower part of Barren Red Measures
Upper 2/3 of Millstone Grit and greater part of Productive Coal Measures

Middle Coal Measures — Lower Coal Measures

(vertical notes:) Many Yorkian species not found or very rare in Pre-Yorkian→ ←Some species restricted to Pre-Yorkian ←Many species common to both

→*Calamites* with ribs on pith casts alternating at nodes

PLANT BREAK:

Calamites← with some ribs alternating at nodes, others passing the nodes without alternating as in *Astero-calamites*

LOWER CARBONIFEROUS

Calciferous Sandstone and Carboniferous Limestone Series

Pitys
Sigillaria very rare.
Lepidodendron abundant, especially *L. veltheimianum* Sternb.
Calamites rare (six species in Britain).
Asterocalamites scrobiculatus (Schl.) occurs throughout.
Pteridosperms represented by many species, belonging especially to the *Sphenopterideae*

Carboniferous Limestone Series
Calamites generally restricted to upper part; *Calamites haueri* Stur, *C. ramifer* Stur, *C. taitana* K. & J.,*Diplotmema adiantoides* (Schl.) (=*Sphenopteris elegans* Brongt.) common.

Calciferous Sandstone Series
Telangium (Sphenopteris) affine (L. & H.) and *Adiantites antiquus* (Ett.) are both confined to this Series.
Diplotmema adiantoides (Schl.) (=Sphenopteris elegans Brongt.) rare.
Rhacopteris sp.
Calamites very rare.

Floral Subdivisions. The basis of the palaeobotanical classification is outlined above. No subdivision of the Lower Carboniferous has been established, but there is evidence for a change of flora at the end of Calciferous Sandstone times, a change which may be correlated with the widespread transgression of the Hurlet Limestone sea. The Upper Carboniferous has been subdivided into four series distinguished mainly by their floral assemblages. Certain species may, however, be restricted to one particular series. Kidston took the dividing line between the pre-Yorkian (his Lanarkian) and the Yorkian (his Westphalian) at the Ell Coal of the Central Coalfield, but Crookall has suggested that it should be drawn at the considerably lower level of the Mill or Auchingane Coal. The upper limit of the Yorkian may be tentatively placed a short distance above Skipsey's Marine Band at the top of the Productive Coal Measures. To the Radstockian are assigned the highest Barren Red Measures of Ayrshire, and a provisional lower limit for this series may be drawn 1,500 ft. or so above Skipsey's Band.

Faunal Subdivisions. In the table on p. 48 (Fig. 10) there have been listed the fossils which have proved of special value for stratigraphical purposes. It will be seen that the index or diagnostic species (those with a narrow vertical range) are few in number. Particular rock-groups or even individual horizons can often be identified, however, by means of their faunal *assemblages*.

Much work has been done in recent years towards establishing zonal successions in the Coal Measures of England, by means of the non-marine lamellibranchs. Davies and Trueman, following up the pioneer work of Wheelton Hind in Staffordshire, established the following descending succession in South Wales (*Quart. Journ. Geol. Soc.*, vol. lxxxiii, pp. 210–257):

> Zone of *Anthracomya tenuis* (now Zone of *Anthraconauta tenuis*).
> Zone of *Anthracomya phillipsi* (now Zone of *Anthraconauta phillipsi*).
> Zone of *Anthracomya pulchra* ⎫ (now Zone of *Anthracosia similis* and
> Zone of *Carbonicola similis* ⎬ *Anthraconaia pulchra*).
> Zone of *Anthracomya modiolaris* (now Zone of *Anthraconaia modiolaris*).
> Zone of *Carbonicola ovalis* (now Zone of *Carbonicola communis*).

This scheme was subsequently extended to the principal English coalfields and a lower portion of the Zone of *Carbonicola communis* [=Zone of *C. ovalis*] separated off to form the Zone of *Anthraconaia (Anthracomya) lenisulcata*. J. Weir and D. Leitch of Glasgow University have investigated the zonal distribution of the non-marine lamellibranchs in the Upper Carboniferous rocks of Scotland and have kindly summarized their results below:

"The Productive Coal Measures of the Central and Ayrshire Coalfields comprise the following zones of Davies and Trueman's scheme:—

> Zone of *Anthracosia similis* and *Anthraconaia pulchra* (lower part).
> Zone of *Anthraconaia modiolaris*.
> Zone of *Carbonicola communis*.

"These zones are represented also in the small outlying coalfield of Douglas, in Lanarkshire, where the occurrence of *Anthraconaia* cf. *bellula* in Millstone

Grit strata suggests that the Zone of *Anthraconaia lenisulcata* may be present in addition.

"A mixed fauna, with forms suggestive of both Communis and Lenisulcata Zones, occurs in the Auldshields Musselband Ironstone, near the base of the Coal Measures in the Airdrie district (Central Coalfield). A similar fauna has been recorded near the top of the Lower Coal Measures of Lancashire, within and near the base of the Communis Zone. The actual base of this zone is indeterminable in Scotland, and no fauna of the Lenisulcata Zone has yet been obtained in the Central Coalfield.

"A conspicuous feature of the faunal succession in the West of Scotland is a subzone of *Carbonicola pseudorobusta*, which, together with the barren strata between the Upper Drumgray and Kiltongue Musselbands, occupies the upper two-thirds of the Communis Zone, and comprises, in the Central Coalfield, the measures between the Mill (or Auchingane) Coal and the Upper Drumgray Coal. The subzone is recognized also in Lancashire, where the entry of its index species, *C. pseudorobusta* Trueman, at the Arley Mine coincides with the boundary between the Lower and Middle Coal Measures. In both Scotland and Lancashire the subzone occupies the same relative position in the general succession, and the Mill Coal may be regarded as at least homotaxially equivalent to the Arley Mine. The greater part of the Productive Coal Measures of the Central Coalfield are therefore of Middle Coal Measure age, only a small fraction, below the Mill Coal, being homotaxially equivalent to the Lower Coal Measures of the North of England. No homotaxial equivalent of the Lower Coal Measures is represented in the Productive Coal Measures of Ayrshire. In North Ayrshire the sediments overlying the Millstone Grit Lavas belong to the Pseudorobusta Sub-Zone, and in South Ayrshire (Dalmellington district) the boundary between Millstone Grit and Coal Measures is taken at the Dalmellington Blackband Ironstone, which marks the entry of *C. pseudorobusta* in that area.

"The base of the Modiolaris Zone is taken at the Kiltongue Musselband in the Central Coalfield and at the Plann Blackband Ironstone in the North Ayrshire Coalfield. The fauna of these undoubtedly equivalent horizons is similar to that of the Trencherbone of Lancashire and the Middleton Main of Yorkshire and marks the entry of such significant forms as *C. os-lancis* Wright and *Anthraconaiae* of the *A. modiolaris* group. This fauna has not up to the present been found in South Ayrshire, where the base of the Modiolaris Zone is taken at the Low Camlarg Coal, following the final occurrence of *C. pseudorobusta* in the Beoch Musselband.

"The base of the Similis-Pulchra Zone is marked by a distinctive fauna, having as its most significant member *Anthraconaia salteri*. This fauna occurs above the Musselband Coal of the Central Coalfield, and above the Three Foot Coal of the Douglas Coalfield; below the Wee (Hurlford Main) Coal of North Ayrshire; and below the Chalmerston of Dalmellington and Diamond of New Cumnock.

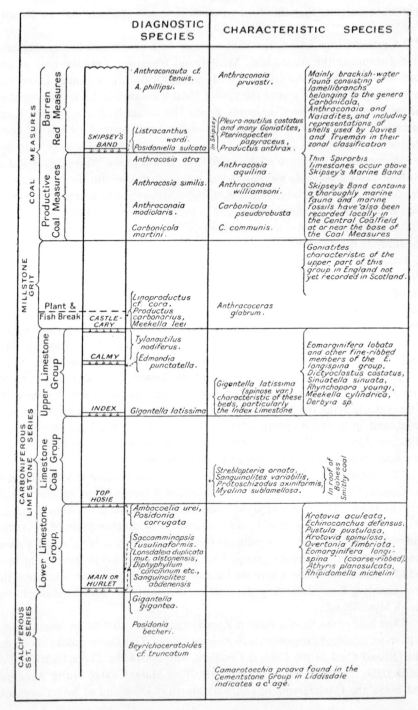

FIG. 10. *Diagram showing horizons of diagnostic and characteristic fossil shells of the Carboniferous of the Midland Valley of Scotland*

"In the Barren Red Measures the Zones of *Anthraconauta phillipsi* and *A. tenuis* have been recognized, the former in the Sanquhar basin and the latter in Central Ayrshire. A fauna of the Phillipsi Zone (*sensu lato*) with *Anthraconaia pruvosti* occurs in the Barren Red Measures of the Clyde at Bothwell.

"In the East of Scotland (Fife and Midlothian) mussel horizons are comparatively rare. In Fife a number of musselbands referable to the lower Similis-Pulchra Zone occurs near the top of the Productive Coal Measures, and the Ovalis zone is represented by a single musselband above the Dysart Main Coal. No faunal representation of the Modiolaris Zone has yet been found. In Midlothian the same two zones have been recognized, but again there is at present no faunal representation of the Modiolaris Zone to record."

SELECTED REFERENCES (STRATIGRAPHY AND PALAEONTOLOGY)

1891. TRAQUAIR, R. H., Fossil Dipnoi and Ganoidei of Fife and the Lothians, *Proc. Roy. Soc. Edin.*, vol. xvii, pp. 385–400.

1901. *The Geology and Palaeontology of the Clyde Drainage Area*, in *Handbook of the Natural History of Glasgow and the West of Scotland*, Brit. Assoc., Glasgow, pp. 399–567; reprinted with corrections and additions by the Geological Society of Glasgow, 1904.

1903. TRAQUAIR, R. H., On the Distribution of Fossil Fish Remains in the Carboniferous Rocks of the Edinburgh District, *Trans. Roy. Soc. Edin.*, vol. xl. part iii, pp. 687–707.

1905. KIDSTON, R., On the Divisions and Correlation of the Upper Portion of the Coal Measures, *Quart. Journ. Geol. Soc.*, vol. lxi, pp. 308–321.

1923. KIDSTON, R., Fossil Plants of the Carboniferous Rocks of Great Britain, Part I (*Mem. Geol. Surv.*), pp. 8, 9, 11, 13.

1925. BAILEY, E. B., in Geology of the Glasgow District (*Mem. Geol. Surv.*), 2nd Edition, pp. 8, 11.

1926. BAILEY, E. B., Subterranean Penetration by a Desert Climate, *Geol. Mag.*, pp. 276–280.

1927. CARRUTHERS, R. G., in Oil-Shales of the Lothians (*Mem. Geol. Surv.*), 3rd Edition, pp. 1–114; this Memoir includes also Sections on Methods of Working the Oil-Shales (W. CALDWELL) and Chemistry and Technology of the Oil-Shales (E. M. BAILEY).

1929. *Handbook of the Geology of Great Britain* (Murby, London); *see* Sections on Lower Carboniferous (E. J. GARWOOD), Millstone Grit (W. B. WRIGHT), and Coal Measures (P. F. KENDALL).

1930. MACGREGOR, M., Scottish Carboniferous Stratigraphy, *Trans. Geol. Soc., Glasgow*, vol. xviii, part iii, pp. 442–558.

1931. CROOKALL, R., A Critical Revision of Kidston's Coal Measure Floras, *Proc. Roy. Physical Soc., Edin.*, vol. xxii, pp. 1–34.

1934. MACGREGOR, M., and J. PRINGLE, The Scottish Millstone Grit and its Position in the Zonal Sequence, in Summary of Progress for 1933, Part II (*Mem. Geol. Surv.*), pp. 1–7.

1936. WEIR, J., and D. LEITCH, Zonal Distribution of the Non-Marine Lamellibranchs in the Coal Measures of Scotland, *Trans. Roy. Soc. Edin.*, vol. lviii, part iii, pp. 697–751.

1937. CURRIE, E. D., C. DUNCAN, and H. M. MUIR-WOOD, The Fauna of Skipsey's Marine Band, *Trans. Geol. Soc. Glasgow*, vol. xix, part iii, pp. 413–452.

1937. WHITE, E. I., The Fishes of the 'Crangopsis Bed' at Ardross, *Geol. Mag.*, pp. 411–428.

1938. MACGREGOR, M., *Conditions of Deposition of the Oil-Shales and Cannel Coals of Scotland*, in *Oil Shale and Cannel Coal, Institute of Petroleum*, London, pp. 6–17.

1938. WALTON, J., J. WEIR, and D. LEITCH, A Summary of Scottish Carboniferous Stratigraphy and Palaeontology, *C. R. 2ième Congr. Stratig. Carbonif.* (Heerlen 1935), pp. 1343–1356.

1939. WRIGHT, J., The Scottish Carboniferous Crinoidea, *Trans. Roy. Soc. Edin.*, vol. lx, part i, pp. 1–78.

1940. LEITCH, D., A Statistical Investigation of the Anthracomyas of the Basal Similis-Pulchra Zone in Scotland, *Quart. Journ. Geol. Soc.*, vol. xcvi, pp. 13–37.

1940. THOMAS, E. G., Revision of the Scottish Carboniferous Pleurotomariidae, *Trans. Geol. Soc. Glasgow*, vol. xx, part i, pp. 30–72.

1941. GORDON, W. T., Salpingostoma dasu: a new Carboniferous seed from East Lothian, *Trans. Roy. Soc. Edin.*, vol. lx, part ii, pp. 427–464.

1941–52. WRIGHT, J., Various Papers on Scottish Crinoids, in *Geol. Mag.* (1941, p. 293; 1942, p. 269; 1944, p. 266; 1945, p. 114; 1946, p. 33; 1948, p. 48; 1952, p. 320).

1942. MACGREGOR, M., The Limestone Coal Group of the Glasgow District, *Wartime Pamphlet* No. 24 (*Geol. Surv.*).

1944. Scottish Coalfields Committee, Scottish Coalfields (*Scottish Home Dept.*).

1945. LEES, G. M., and A. H. TAITT, The Geological Results of the Search for Oilfields in Great Britain, *Quart. Journ. Geol. Soc.*, vol. ci, pp. 255–317.

1945. MACGREGOR, A. G., The Mineral Resources of the Lothians, *Wartime Pamphlet No.* 45 (*Geol. Surv.*).

1945. MACGREGOR, M., The Mineral Resources of Scotland, *Proc. Roy. Phil. Soc. Glasgow*, vol. lxx, part iii, pp. 27–42.

1945. WEIR, J., A Review of the Recent Work on the Permian Non-marine Lamellibranchs and its Bearing on the affinities of certain Non-marine Genera of the Upper Palaeozoic, *Trans. Geol. Soc. Glasgow*, vol. xx, part iii, pp. 291–340.

1946. MACLENNAN, R. M., The Carbonicola Fauna of the Ovalis Zone in Scotland, *Trans. Geol. Soc. Glasgow*, vol. xxi, part i, pp. 75–96.

1946–7. TRUEMAN, A. E., and J. WEIR, A Monograph of British Carboniferous Non-marine Lamellibranchia, *Mon. Pal. Soc.*, parts i and ii.

See also List of Geological Survey Memoirs on p. 94; a number of these contain extensive bibliographies.

IGNEOUS ROCKS: PETROLOGY

Throughout much of the period during which the sediments of the Carboniferous System were being deposited, an area of intense volcanic activity was located in Central and Southern Scotland. The stratigraphical range of the contemporaneous igneous rocks, which form extensive areas of hill-country (pp. 2, 3), is shown in Fig. 11 (52).

Numerous basic intrusive sills are found in the Carboniferous rocks; they represent subterranean injection of molten magma that accompanied surface eruptions. The prolongation of volcanic activity into Permian times makes it difficult to assign a definite age to many of these sills, for the Permian and basic Carboniferous magmas had many points of similarity. Intrusions to which a

LOCAL SEQUENCES OF VOLCANIC ROCKS OF CALCIFEROUS SANDSTONE AGE

Kilbirnie Hills (Greenock–Ardrossan Uplands South of Knockside Hills)	Beith–Eaglesham–Strathaven Uplands	Campsie Fells	East Lothian (Garleton Hills District)
Volcanic detritus (Calciferous Sandstone Series)	*Volcanic detritus (Calciferous Sandstone Series)*	*Volcanic detritus (Calciferous Sandstone Series)*	*Volcanic detritus (Calciferous Sandstone Series)*
UNCONFORMITY	UNCONFORMITY	UNCONFORMITY	UNCONFORMITY
3.* Rhyolite lava (local), and trachytic vent-agglomerate (Knockside Hills) cut by trachytic and some basaltic intrusions.	5.* Trachyte, trachyandesite and some trachybasalt lavas, with associated trachytic tuffs. Trachytic plugs.	4. Trachytic vent-agglomerate (Meikle Bin) cut by trachytic and some basaltic intrusions.	3. Trachyte and quartz-banakite lavas, with trachytic tuff interbedded locally. Trachytic plugs.
2. Markle basalts with subordinate mugearites, and some local flows of Jedburgh, Dalmeny and Dunsapie basalt.	4. Dalmeny, Dalmeny - Dunsapie, and Jedburgh basalts, with mugearites locally.	3. Markle basalts and mugearites.	2. Markle, Dunsapie, and Craiglockhart basalts, with some flows of mugearite and of kulaite.
1. Basaltic tuff (local).	3.* Trachyte, trachyandesite and rhyolite lavas, with trachytic tuffs associated locally.	2. Jedburgh basalts.	1. Basaltic tuff.
Upper Old Red Sandstone.	2. Dalmeny and Jedburgh basalts, with mugearites locally.	1. Basaltic tuff (local).	*Sediments of Calciferous Sandstone Series.*
	1. Markle and Dunsapie basalts, with local Craiglockhart Dalmeny basalts.	*Sediments of Calciferous Sandstone Series, or (locally) of Upper Old Red Sandstone.*	
	Base not seen.		

* These trachytic and rhyolitic lavas and tuffs are strictly localized, and occur only near some of the numerous trachytic plugs or vents. Pebbles of acid rocks in the volcanic detritus may indicate, however, that the trachytic rocks originally had a wider extent.

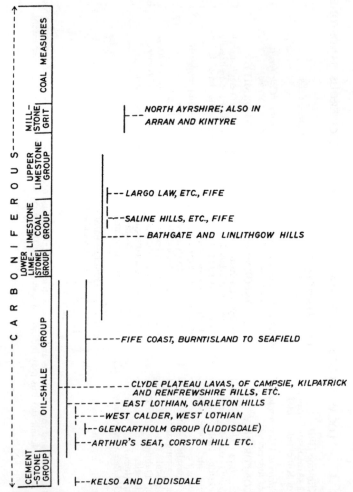

DIAGRAM TO SHOW
STRATIGRAPHICAL RANGE OF
CHIEF VOLCANIC EPISODES

FIG. 11. *Diagram showing stratigraphical range of chief volcanic episodes in the Carboniferous of the Midland Valley and Southern Uplands of Scotland. Recent evidence suggests a higher horizon (possibly Millstone Grit) for volcanic rocks at Largo Law.*

Carboniferous age cannot be definitely assigned are accordingly treated in a later section, along with similar rocks of Permian age.

The Carboniferous intrusions considered here occur chiefly as ash-necks, and as vent-intrusions, plugs, or dykes, of various petrographical types similar to those found among the lava-form rocks, in or near which they occur. It is noteworthy, however, that phonolites and phonolitic trachytes are found only as intrusions. Some of the less basic rocks form large sills or laccoliths. Intrusions of plutonic character are unknown.

The Midland Valley in Carboniferous times formed part[1] of a petrographical province in which the eruptive rocks belong to the alkaline (sodic) magma series. In some areas the earlier basaltic lavas were succeeded towards the end of the Calciferous Sandstone volcanic activity by leucocratic alkaline and acid rocks, which occur in the form of lavas, ashes or intrusions (Table, p. 51). Olivine-rich basalt lavas were, however, poured out again in Carboniferous Limestone times, as a continuation of the Calciferous Sandstone vulcanicity, in Fife and in the Bathgate Hills (West Lothian), and at the close of Millstone Grit times in Ayrshire. Basalt intrusions also cut the agglomerate of some of the trachytic vents.

Olivine-basalt Lavas are by far the most abundant of Carboniferous flows; they have been divided, for mapping purposes, into a 'macroporphyritic' group with conspicuous phenocrysts, and a 'microporphyritic' group with inconspicuous phenocrysts (Table, p. 54). The alkaline affinities of the basalts are indicated by the fact that analcite is an accessory mineral of frequent occurrence.

Markle basalts are abundantly represented in all the districts where lavas are found, with the exception of Fifeshire, the Bathgate Hills and the Central Ayrshire Coalfield. They are often associated with mugearites or with Jedburgh basalts. Composite flows consisting of an upper porphyritic layer of Markle basalt and a lower non-porphyritic layer of basaltic mugearite have recently been described from near Greenock (Kennedy, 1931). *Dunsapie basalts* are well represented only in East Lothian and in the Kilpatrick Hills. *Craiglockhart basalts* are fairly numerous in East Lothian; a few flows occur elsewhere. *Jedburgh basalts* are most abundant in the Campsie Fells. *Dalmeny basalts* are prevalent in Fife (Burntisland and Kinghorn) and the Bathgate Hills, and are well represented in the Edinburgh–Lanark district and the Beith–Eaglesham–Strathaven uplands; in the latter area they are associated with a widely developed series of flows transitional between the Dalmeny and Dunsapie types. The few lavas that represent Calciferous Sandstone volcanic activity in the Central Ayrshire Coalfield, as well as practically all the Millstone Grit lavas of Ayrshire, and of Fife (Allan and Knox, 1934), belong to the Dalmeny type. *Hillhouse*

---

[1] Carboniferous lavas and intrusions are found in parts of the Southern Uplands, notably near Kelso and in Teviotdale and Liddisdale, and in Arran and Kintyre.

TABLE SHOWING MINERAL CONSTITUENTS OF SCOTTISH CARBONIFEROUS OLIVINE-BASALTS

ROCK NAME	PHENOCRYSTS or PORPHYRITIC CRYSTALS (Relatively large crystals set in a matrix of much smaller ones)	Constituents of the matrix or GROUNDMASS in which the phenocrysts are embedded			NOTES ON OCCURRENCE OF TYPE ROCK
		Always present	Often present	Sometimes present	
MACROPORPHYRITIC GROUP (Many phenocrysts are more than 2 mm. in length)					
OLIVINE-BASALT OF MARKLE TYPE	Labradorite feldspar Olivine (small in type rock)	Labradorite Augite Iron-ore	Orthoclase Oligoclase Olivine Chlorite Apatite	Biotite Brown hornblende	Lava flow Markle Quarry, East Lothian
OLIVINE-BASALT OF DUNSAPIE TYPE	Labradorite feldspar Olivine Augite	Labradorite Augite Iron-ore	Oligoclase Olivine, Analcite Chlorite Apatite	Biotite Brown hornblende Glass Chlorophaeite	Intrusion in vent Dunsapie Hill, Holyrood Park, Edinburgh
OLIVINE-BASALT OF CRAIGLOCKHART TYPE	Olivine Augite	Labradorite Augite Iron-ore	Olivine Chlorite Apatite		Lava flow Craiglockhart Hill, Edinburgh
MICROPORPHYRITIC GROUP (Phenocrysts are less than 2 mm. in length)					
OLIVINE-BASALT OF JEDBURGH TYPE	Labradorite feldspar Olivine	Labradorite Augite Iron-ore (Flow structure of feldspar laths is characteristic)	Orthoclase Oligoclase Analcite Chlorite Apatite	Biotite Brown hornblende Glass	Plug in vent Little Caldon, Stirlingshire (Similar rocks form plugs near Jedburgh, Roxburghshire)
OLIVINE-BASALT OF DALMENY TYPE	Olivine (With, sometimes, sporadic labradorites and augites)	Labradorite Augite Iron-ore	Chlorite Analcite Apatite	Oligoclase Biotite Glass Chlorophaeite	Lava flow Near Dalmeny Church, West Lothian
OLIVINE-BASALT OF HILLHOUSE TYPE	Olivine Augite (not always present)	Augite, iron-ore and a little labradorite, with analcite or glass	Chlorite	Biotite Apatite	Sill Hillhouse Quarry, West Lothian

TRACHYANDESITES, TRACHYTES AND RHYOLITES

	ROCK NAME	PHENOCRYSTS or PORPHYRITIC CRYSTALS (Relatively large crystals set in a matrix of much smaller ones)		Constituents of the matrix or GROUNDMASS in which the phenocrysts are embedded	REMARKS ON MICROSCOPIC CHARACTERS
		Usually present	Sometimes present		
TRACHYBASALTS	MUGEARITE	None	Plagioclase feldspar Alkali feldspar Olivine Augite	Dominantly feldspathic; structure usually trachytic	Typically non-porphyritic and very fine-grained. Flow-structure of feldspar laths almost always very pronounced.
TRACHYBASALTS	KULAITE	Brown hornblende* Augite	Olivine	Oligoclase, iron-ore, olivine and/or augite, with subordinate biotite, brown hornblende, chlorite, chlorophaeite, glass, analcite.	Augite greyish-fawn to faintly purplish. No flow-structure. Original leucites (groundmass) replaced by analcite.
TRACHYBASALTS	OTHER TRACHYBASALTS	Plagioclase feldspar Augite Olivine	Brown hornblende*	Oligoclase with subordinate orthoclase, and some analcite, augite, iron-ore, olivine, biotite and apatite.	Plagioclase phenocrysts (e.g. labradorite) often mantled and penetrated by oligoclase or alkali feldspar. Augite phenocrysts purplish, sometimes with a green core.
TRACHYANDE-SITES	QUARTZ-BANAKITE	Plagioclase feldspar Augite	Alkali feldspar Olivine	Plagioclase (oligoclase to labradorite) and alkali feldspar, with some augite, olivine, iron-ore and apatite. Groundmass more calcic or mafic than in trachyandesites.	Plagioclase phenocrysts (e.g. labradorite) mantled and penetrated by orthoclase. Augite a green soda-bearing variety.
TRACHYANDE-SITES	OTHER TRACHYANDESITES	Plagioclase feldspar Augite Olivine	Alkali feldspar Brown hornblende*	Orthoclase with some augite, iron-ore, and sparse interstitial quartz. Plagioclase (oligoclase to labradorite) and/or alkali feldspar, with some augite, olivine, iron-ore, biotite, chlorite, chlorophaeite, and apatite. Resorbed hornblende in the hornblende-trachyandesites.	Plagioclase phenocrysts (albite-oligoclase to labradorite) often mantled and penetrated by alkali feldspar or oligoclase. Augite phenocrysts greyish-fawn to purplish.
	PHONOLITE and PHONOLITIC TRACHYTE		Plagioclase feldspar Alkali feldspar Augite Olivine (fayalite) Brown hornblende*	Albitic plagioclase and alkali feldspar with augite, olivine (fayalite), iron-ore, nepheline, analcite, apatite, and sometimes sodalite. Nepheline may occur in groundmass, or as enclosures in feldspar phenocrysts.	Alkali feldspar phenocrysts (orthoclase or anorthoclase) sometimes have a core of plagioclase. Augite often a green soda-bearing variety.
	TRACHYTE	Alkali feldspar	Augite Brown hornblende* Olivine (very rare)	Alkali feldspar, with some augite, iron-ore and apatite. Interstitial quartz may also be present. Note.—Soda-amphibole occurs in some trachytes in Southern Scotland (Tweeddale and Teviotdale).	Alkali feldspar phenocrysts are orthoclase anorthoclase, or albite-rich plagioclase. Augite may be a green soda-bearing variety.
	RHYOLITE and FELSITE	Alkali feldspar	Augite	Minute alkali feldspars set in a quartz base, with sparse iron-ore.	Alkali feldspar, phenocrysts are orthoclase, anorthoclase, or albite-rich plagioclase. Sparse ferromagnesian phenocrysts usually quite decomposed. These rocks are usually much decomposed throughout.

* Often resorbed, or partly resorbed.

basalts are almost confined to Fife and the Bathgate Hills, where they are well represented.

Trachybasalt Lavas. *Mugearites* (Table, p. 55) are found everywhere, except in Fife, the Bathgate Hills and the Central Ayrshire Coalfield, but in bulk they are very subordinate to the basalts. Other types of *trachybasalt* occur locally in the Eaglesham uplands, while the hornblende-bearing *leucīte-kulaites* are represented by four flows in East Lothian; in these rocks the leucite has been replaced by analcite (Bennet, 1945).

Trachyandesite, Trachyte and Rhyolite Lavas. *Hornblende-trachyandesites* are confined to the Dunlop–Eaglesham–Strathaven uplands. Other types of trachyandesite are also abundant in the same area (Plate V and Fig. 14), and one flow is known near Kilmacolm, between Greenock and Paisley (Kennedy, 1933). Trachytic lavas cover considerable areas in East Lothian (Figs. 12 and 13) and in the Dunlop–Eaglesham–Strathaven uplands; in the eastern area there are *trachytes* and *quartz-banakites*, while in the western district the trachyandesites already mentioned are associated with trachytes and some *rhyolites*. One rhyolite lava is known in the hills north of Ardrossan, and three flows of trachyte in Bute.

Zeolites, etc. The Carboniferous volcanic rocks of the Midland Valley, especially in the Campsie and Kilpatrick Hills and the Renfrewshire uplands, have long been famous as a source of beautiful specimens of minerals of the zeolite group, and of the allied minerals *apophyllite*, *prehnite* and *pectolite*.

The zeolites and allied minerals are found locally filling cavities or vesicles, or forming veins, in vent-intrusions or in slaggy lavas. They were deposited during the later stages of consolidation of the igneous rocks in which they occur.

Basaltic Tuffs. In all districts where the base of the Calciferous Sandstone sequence of volcanic rocks is exposed basaltic tuffs occur at this horizon or a little above it. Tuffs intercalated at higher levels in the Carboniferous sequence are comparatively rare, except among the lava-flows of the Bathgate Hills, and in Fife.

Trachytic Tuffs are associated with the trachytic lavas of East Lothian and of the Eaglesham–Darvel district. In the latter area the outcrops are extensive and some of the material is coarse agglomerate with blocks of trachyte up to several feet in diameter.

Basaltic Necks. Volcanic necks filled with *basaltic agglomerate*, often accompanied by basic vent-intrusions, are widely distributed throughout most of the volcanic districts (Plates VI and VIIB). They are the denuded stumps of the volcanoes from which the basaltic lavas were erupted, and often stand up as prominent hills. The necks usually have a circular or oval outline and rarely exceed a quarter of a mile in diameter. One of the most famous is Arthur's Seat,

Edinburgh (Plate IIIB), about half a mile across. Other notable examples are the Saline Hills (Haldane, 1931), the Binn Hill of Burntisland and Largo Law in Fife,

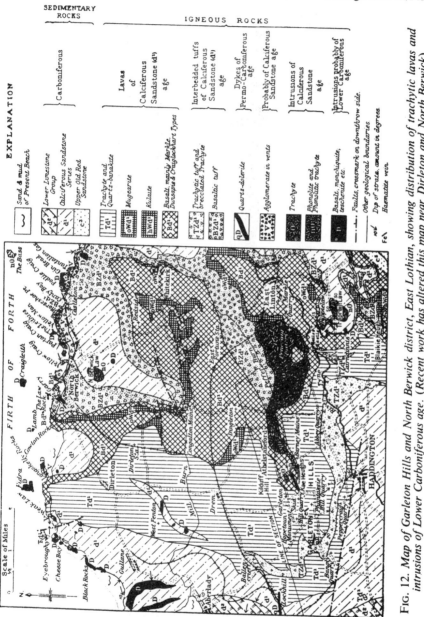

FIG. 12. Map of Garleton Hills and North Berwick district, East Lothian, showing distribution of trachytic lavas and intrusions of Lower Carboniferous age. (Recent work has altered this map near Dirleton and North Berwick)

Dunsyre Hill between West Linton and Lanark, Dumgoyn and Dumfoyn at the west end of the Campsie Fells, and the Heads of Ayr on the shore of the Firth

E

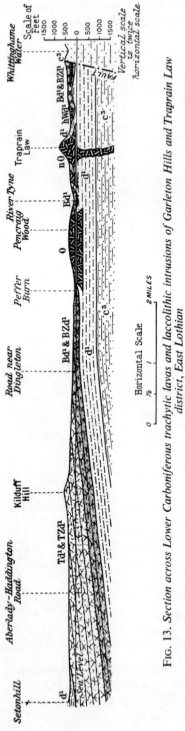

FIG. 13. *Section across Lower Carboniferous trachytic lavas and laccolithic intrusions of Garleton Hills and Traprain Law district, East Lothian*

c^3= Upper Old Red Sandstone; Carboniferous: d^1= Calciferous Sandstone Series, Bd^1= basalt lava, BZd^1= basaltic tuff, hWd^1= kulaite lava, Td^1= trachyte and quartz-banakite lavas, TZd^1= trachytic tuff, O= trachyte laccolith, nO= phonolite laccolith

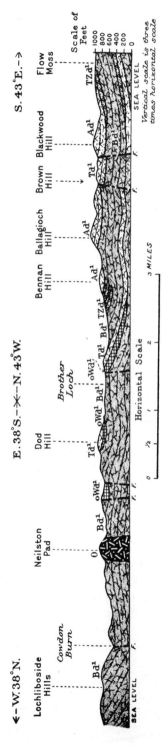

Fig. 14. *Section across part of the Clyde Carboniferous lava plateau illustrating relations of the trachytic rocks to the basalt lavas*

Carboniferous: Bd^1=basalt lava, oWd^1=mugearite lava, Ad^1=trachyandesite lava, Td^1=trachyte lava, TZd^1=trachyte and rhyolite lavas, TZd^1=trachytic tuff, O=trachyte plug, F=fault

of Clyde (Eyles, 1929). Numerous vents which are probably all of Lower Carboniferous age (p. 69) are seen in section on the south shore of the Firth of Forth near North Berwick (Day, 1923–32) and Dunbar, while in the west a remarkable line of vents of the Calciferous Sandstone period extends for two and a half miles along the base of lavas of the Campsie Fells north-east of Strath Blane. Notable examples of *necks completely filled with basalt* are the Castle Rock in Edinburgh, Dungoil, Dunglass and Dumgoyach in the Campsie Fells area north of Glasgow, and Dumbarton Rock on the River Clyde. The basic intrusions in the necks are usually basalts of types corresponding to those found among the lava-flows. Basalt of Hillhouse type is fairly common as a vent-intrusion, even in districts where it rarely forms surface flows.

Trachytic Necks. Volcanic necks filled with *trachytic agglomerate* are not numerous. Small occurrences are known in East Lothian, in the Kilbirnie Hills and between Strathaven and Darvel. Meikle Bin in the Campsie Fells, an oval vent one and a half miles long, is perhaps the best example. The great area of trachytic ash, etc., around Misty Law and the Knockside Hills, in the centre of the Greenock–Ardrossan uplands, is much larger; it is believed to contain trachytic lavas and to represent a large caldera ('Summary of Progress for 1937,' *Mem. Geol. Surv.*, 1938, p. 66).

Two *plugs of trachytic rock* occur in East Lothian; these are the phonolitic trachytes of the Bass Rock and of North Berwick Law. In the Beith–Eaglesham–Strathaven uplands the basalt lavas are cut by no less than ten plugs of trachy-andesite or trachyte (*e.g.* Loudoun Hill, Neilston Pad, Lochlands Hill) and by five plugs of phonolitic trachyte (*e.g.* Underlaw near Darvel, Laird's Seat, and Townhead of Grange near Lugton). Trachytic vent-intrusions occur also in the agglomerate of the Knockside Hills and in the adjacent Great Cumbrae Island in the Firth of Clyde.

Dykes, Sills, etc. The Carboniferous dykes are as a rule narrow (12 ft. or less) and can rarely be traced across country for any distance. In a few instances, as in the Great Cumbrae, dykes of basalt attain 40 ft. and dykes of trachyte 50 ft. or even 100 ft. in width.

Basaltic Dykes and Sills. *Basic dykes* and *sills* corresponding to the basalt lava types are, as a rule, not very abundant. Dykes of Markle basalt are, however, well represented in the Campsie Fells, and in the Great Cumbrae where they are associated with many of Dunsapie type. Dykes of Jedburgh basalt occur in the Kilpatrick Hills and in the Great Cumbrae. Craiglockhart and Dalmeny basalts occur very rarely in the form of dykes. The most notable *basaltic sill* is that of St. Leonard's Craig, Edinburgh, a composite intrusion in which the central porphyritic portion is very rich in analcite, but otherwise resembles a Dunsapie basalt. Another well-known basic sill, near Linlithgow, is the type occurrence of Hillhouse basalt. Three sills of Markle basalt have been recorded in Bute.

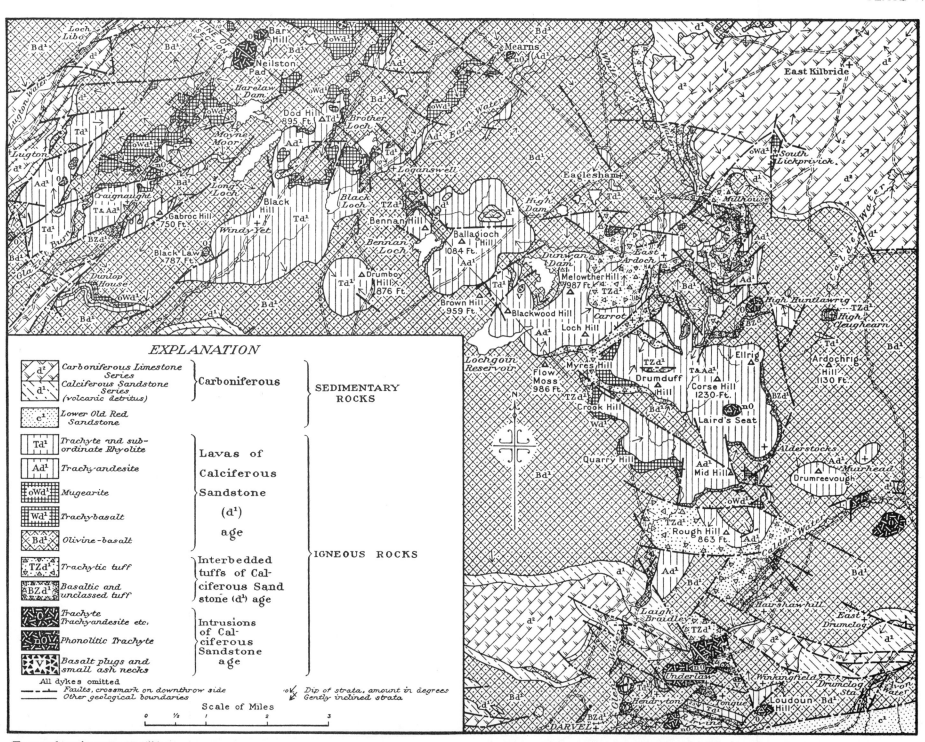

EXPLANATION

d²	Carboniferous Limestone Series	
d¹	Calciferous Sandstone Series (volcanic detritus)	Carboniferous

SEDIMENTARY ROCKS

c¹	Lower Old Red Sandstone	

Td¹	Trachyte and subordinate Rhyolite	
Ad¹	Trachyandesite	Lavas of Calciferous Sandstone (d¹) age
oWd¹	Mugearite	
Wd¹	Trachybasalt	
Bd¹	Olivine-basalt	

IGNEOUS ROCKS

TZd¹	Trachytic tuff	Interbedded tuffs of Calciferous Sandstone (d¹) age
BZd¹	Basaltic and unclassed tuff	
O	Trachyte Trachyandesite etc.	Intrusions of Calciferous Sandstone age
nO	Phonolitic Trachyte	
V	Basalt plugs and small ash necks	

All dykes omitted

- - - - Faults, crossmark on downthrow side
———— Other geological boundaries

Dip of strata, amount in degrees
Gently inclined strata

Scale of Miles
0   ½   1   2   3

(For explanation, *see* p. vii.)

MAP OF PART OF CLYDE LAVA PLATEAU IN RENFREWSHIRE, NORTH AYRSHIRE AND LANARKSHIRE

Mugearite dykes are sparse, but isolated examples have been recorded from the Kilpatrick Hills, the Greenock–Ardrossan uplands and Great Cumbrae Island. Two *hornblende-trachybasalt* dykes are known in the uplands north-east of Beith.

Trachytic Dykes and Sills. *Felsite* or *trachyte dykes* are abundant in and around the trachytic agglomerate of the Meikle Bin vent in the Campsie Fells, and that of the Knockside Hills–Misty Law centre in the Greenock–Ardrossan uplands. There are many similar dykes in the Great Cumbrae.

Two large *laccolithic sills of trachyte* occur in East Lothian (Pencraig and Garvald). The dome shape of Traprain Law, in the same district, is due to the laccolithic form of this intrusion of *phonolite*. A well-known trachyte sill in western Scotland is that of Craigmushet, at Gourock, Renfrewshire. Other *trachytic* and *felsitic sills* of Carboniferous age cut the Upper Old Red sandstones that fringe the eastern shore of the Firth of Clyde from Inverkip to Ardrossan and extend into the Great Cumbrae Island. Two trachytic intrusions of unknown form cut Calciferous Sandstone sediments just below the lavas of the Campsie Fells; one of these is the well-known *phonolite* of Fintry.

MAIN OUTCROPS AND SELECTED REFERENCES (IGNEOUS ROCKS)
General.
1897. GEIKIE, Sir A., *The Ancient Volcanoes of Great Britain*, vol. i (Macmillan, London), pp. 355–477.
1928. MACGREGOR, A. G., The Classification of Scottish Carboniferous Olivine-basalts and Mugearites, *Trans. Geol. Soc. Glasgow*, vol. xviii, part ii, pp. 324–360. This paper contains a comprehensive bibliography.
1928. RICHEY, J. E., The North Ayrshire Sequence of Calciferous Sandstone Volcanic Rocks, *Trans. Geol. Soc. Glasgow*, vol. xviii, part ii, pp. 255–257.
1931. GUPPY, E. M., and H. H. THOMAS, Chemical Analyses of Igneous Rocks, Metamorphic Rocks and Minerals (*Mem. Geol. Surv.*), pp. 15, 17, 19, 24–28, 42–44, 66–73, 76, 79–81, 87, 99.
1935. TURNER, J. S., A Review of Dinantian and Namurian Vulcanicity in North-western and Central Europe, *Geol. Mag.*, pp. 458–470.
1937. MACGREGOR, A. G., The Carboniferous and Permian Volcanoes of Scotland, *Bull. Volcanol.*, Sér. ii, tome i, pp. 41–58.
1937. TOMKEIEFF, S. I., Petrochemistry of the Scottish Carboniferous-Permian Igneous Rocks, *Bull. Volcanol.*, Sér. ii, tome i, pp. 59–87.
1939. RICHEY, J. E., The Dykes of Scotland, *Trans. Edin. Geol. Soc.*, vol. xiii, part iv, pp. 411–413.
Fife.
1923. BALSILLIE, D., Further Observations on the Volcanic Geology of East Fife, *Geol. Mag.*, pp. 530–542.
1924. ALLAN, D. A., The Igneous Geology of the Buntisland District, *Trans. Royal Soc. Edin.*, vol. liii, part iii, pp. 479–502.
1927. BALSILLIE, D., Contemporaneous Volcanic Activity in East Fife, *Geol. Mag.*, pp. 481–494.
1928. CUMMING, G. A., The Lower Limestones and Associated Volcanic Rocks of a Section of the Fifeshire Coast, *Trans. Edin. Geol. Soc.*, vol. xii, part i, pp. 134–135.

1931. HALDANE, D., and J. K. ALLAN, The Economic Geology of the Fife Coalfields, Area I (*Mem. Geol. Surv.*), pp. 5, 66–68.
1934. ALLAN, J. K., and J. KNOX, in The Economic Geology of the Fife Coalfields, Area II (*Mem. Geol. Surv.*), pp. 6, 181.
1936. CUMMING, C. A., The Structural and Volcanic Geology of the Elie–St. Monance District, Fife, *Trans. Edin. Geol. Soc.*, vol. xiii, part iii, pp. 340–365.
1936. DAVIES, L. M., The Geology of Inchkeith, *Trans. Roy. Soc. Edin.*, vol. lviii, part iii, pp. 753–786.

Bathgate Hills: West Lothian.
1910. FLETT, J. S., in Geology of the Neighbourhood of Edinburgh (*Mem. Geol. Surv.*), pp. 144–156 and 317.

East Lothian: including Garleton Hills.
1910. BAILEY, E. B., and others, in The Geology of East Lothian (*Mem. Geol. Surv.*), pp. 69–133.
1922. MACGREGOR, A. G., and F. R. ENNOS, The Traprain Law Phonolite, *Geol. Mag.*, pp. 514–523.
1923–1932. DAY, T. C., Various Papers in *Trans. Edin. Geol. Soc.*, vols. xi and xii.
1934. CAMPBELL, R., and A. G. STENHOUSE, The Occurrence of Nepheline and Fayalite in the Phonolitic Trachyte of the Bass Rock, *Trans. Edin. Geol. Soc.*, vol. xiii, part i, pp. 126–132.
1945. BENNET, J. A. E., Some Occurences of Leucite in East Lothian, *Trans. Edin. Geol. Soc.*, vol. xiv, part i, pp. 34–52.

Edinburgh–Lanark District.
1910. FLETT, J. S., and others, in Geology of the Neighbourhood of Edinburgh (*Mem. Geol. Surv.*), pp. 54–75, 316–323.
1921. PEACH, B. N., and Sir J. S. FLETT, in Description of Arthur's Seat Volcano (*Mem. Geol. Surv.*), 2nd Edition.
1926. RICHEY, J. E., and J. PHEMISTER, in Summary of Progress for 1925 (*Mem. Geol. Surv.*), pp. 108–109.
1933. DAY, T. C., Arthur's Seat (Oliver and Boyd, Edinburgh).
1934. MACGREGOR, A. G., The Composite Sill of St. Leonard's Craig and Heriot Mount, Edinburgh, *Trans. Edin. Geol. Soc.*, vol. xiii, part iii, pp. 317–331.

Camspie Fells (with Gargunnock Hills) and Kilpatrick Hills.
1913. TYRRELL, G. W., The Petrology of the Kilpatrick Hills, Dumbartonshire, *Trans. Geol. Soc., Glasgow*, vol. xiv, part iii, pp. 219–257.
1925. BAILEY, E. B., and others, in The Geology of the Glasgow District (*Mem. Geol. Surv.*), 2nd Edition, pp. 135–149, 175–185.
1927. DINHAM, C. H., Stirling District, *Proc. Geol. Assoc.*, vol. xxxviii, pp. 472–473.
1930. SIMPSON, J. B., in Summary of Progress for 1929, Part i (*Mem. Geol. Surv.*), p. 74.
1938. DIXON, C. G., The Geology of the Fintry, Gargunnock and Touch Hills, *Geol. Mag.*, pp. 425–432.

Greenock-Ardrossan Uplands.
1917. LEITCH, P. A., and A. SCOTT, Notes on the Intrusive Rocks of West Renfrewshire, *Trans. Geol. Soc. Glasgow*, vol. xvi, part ii, pp. 275–289.
1928. RICHEY, J. E., The North Ayrshire Sequence of Calciferous Sandstone Volcanic Rocks, *Trans. Geol. Soc. Glasgow*, vol. xviii, part ii, pp. 247–255.

1930. RICHEY, J. E., G. V. WILSON and A. G. MACGREGOR, in The Geology of North Ayrshire (*Mem. Geol. Surv.*), pp. 64–69, 83–88, 89–131.
1930. MACGREGOR, A. G., and W. Q. KENNEDY, in Summary of Progress for 1929, Part I (*Mem. Geol. Surv.*), pp. 72–73.
1931. KENNEDY, W. Q., On Composite Lava Flows, *Geol. Mag.*, pp. 166–181.
1933. KENNEDY, W. Q., Composite Auto-intrusion in a Carboniferous Lava Flow, Summary of Progress for 1932, Part II (*Mem Geol. Surv.*), pp. 83–93.

Bute and Cumbrae Islands: Firth of Clyde.

1916. SMELLIE, W. R., The Igneous Rocks of Bute, *Trans. Geol. Soc. Glasgow*, vol. xv, part iii, pp. 334–373.
1917. TYRRELL, G. W., The Igneous Geology of the Cumbrae Islands, *op. cit.*, vol. xvi, part ii, pp. 244–274.
1940. McCALLIEN, W. J., Notes on the Geological Structure of South Bute, *Trans. Geol. Soc. Glasgow*, vol. xx, part i, pp. 96–102.

Beith–Eaglesham–Strathaven–Uplands.

1917. TYRRELL, G. W., The Trachytic and Allied Rocks of the Clyde Carboniferous Lava-Plateaus, *Proc. Royal Soc. Edin.*, vol. xxxvi, pp. 288–299.
1924–25. PHEMISTER, J., in Summary of Progress for 1923, p. 105 and in Summary of Progress for 1924, pp. 104–105 (*Mems. Geol. Surv.*).
1928. RICHEY, J. E., The North Ayrshire Sequence of Calciferous Sandstone Volcanic Rocks, *Trans. Geol. Soc. Glasgow*, vol. xviii, part ii, pp. 247–255.
1930. RICHEY, J. E., and A. G. MACGREGOR, in The Geology of North Ayrshire (*Mem. Geol. Surv.*), pp. 64–131.

Central Ayrshire Coalfield.

1922. WILSON, G. V., The Ayrshire Bauxitic Clay (*Mem. Geol. Surv.*).
1929. EYLES, V. A., and others, The Igneous Geology of Central Ayrshire, *Trans. Geol. Soc. Glasgow*, vol. xviii, part iii, pp. 369–374. (*See also* Geology of Central Ayrshire, *Mem. Geol. Surv.*, Chapters v and vii).
1930. BAILEY, E. B., and others, in The Geology of North Ayrshire (*Mem. Geol. Surv.*), pp. 60–61, 177–180, 197–224.
1930. EYLES, V. A., and J. B. SIMPSON, in The Economic Geology of the Ayrshire Coalfields, Area III (*Mem. Geol. Surv.*), pp. 63–73.

VI. TESCHENITIC, THERALITIC AND MONCHIQUITIC INTRUSIONS OF CARBONIFEROUS AND PERMIAN TIMES

A LARGE number of basic analcite-bearing sills are found in the Midland Valley of Scotland (Plate VI). The great majority cut sedimentary rocks of Carboniferous age and are localized in four districts: (1) Fife; (2) The Lothians; (3) The Glasgow District; (4) The Ayrshire Coalfield.

For descriptive purposes these olivine-bearing intrusions may be grouped (Table, p. 65) as Kylitic types, Teschenitic types, Monchiquitic types, Doleritic and Basaltic types, and altered Doleritic types. As different schemes of classification are current, a few notes must be given to clarify the nomenclature adopted here.

The few Kylitic types occurring in eastern Scotland have been described as teschenites. Fresh olivine-rich rocks allied to the type kylite of Tyrell are abundant in Central Ayrshire and have certain common characteristics which give them individuality both in the field and under the microscope (Table, p. 65). As these rocks rarely occur in the same intrusive body as teschenitic types (*sensu stricto*), it is useful to distinguish them by a group name.

With the teschenitic types are grouped certain rocks called essexites by Bailey (Craigleith), Flett (Lochend) and Balsillie (Fife), and coarse ophitic analcite-bearing alkaline olivine-dolerites from Ayrshire, classed as 'crinanites' by Tyrrell, and possibly of Tertiary age. Crinanites are not specifically included in the Table; they are, however, very similar to ophitic augite-teschenites. Teschenites may be coarse and ophitic or fine-grained ('basaltic') and intergranular. The finer-grained rocks, which are almost confined to Fife, where they are abundant, approach analcite-basanites in character.

Similar variations occur in the olivine-bearing Doleritic and Basaltic types, which contain very little analcite. These are well developed in Fife, where they sometimes occur as local facies of teschenitic sills.

Among the altered Doleritic types are included rocks of different kinds which have been very considerably changed by deuteric (late-magmatic) agencies. Some contain quartz and in others olivine has not been found; they are considered here because of the close association of some of them with teschenitic types.

Kylitic Types are well developed in the Kyle district of Ayrshire north of Dalmellington. The type kylite of Benbeoch, an olivine-rich theralitic essexite (Tyrrell, 1912), is part of a thick sill which forms several neighbouring outliers. Other sills occur at Craigs of Kyle and near High Mount, Skares, and Dundonald. In those outcrops there occur varieties both less basic and more basic than the type rock, and locally picrite is found; a felsic alkaline 'segregation' vein has been recorded. The details of the mineralogical variation in the sills are not yet known, but the grain-size varies considerably, the finer-grained varieties approaching basaltic texture. Coarse ('doleritic') bands containing large augites, have been recorded.

The kylitic sills of Ayrshire are at present extensively quarried for road-metal.

A rather coarse-grained essexite or theralite with large augites forms a small intrusion in the Permian neck of Carclout near Patna, Ayrshire; it closely resembles the well-known essexite plug or boss of Lennoxtown. The latter is the only rock of kylitic type known in the Glasgow district. One or two kylitic dykes occur near Carskeoch Hill, Patna.

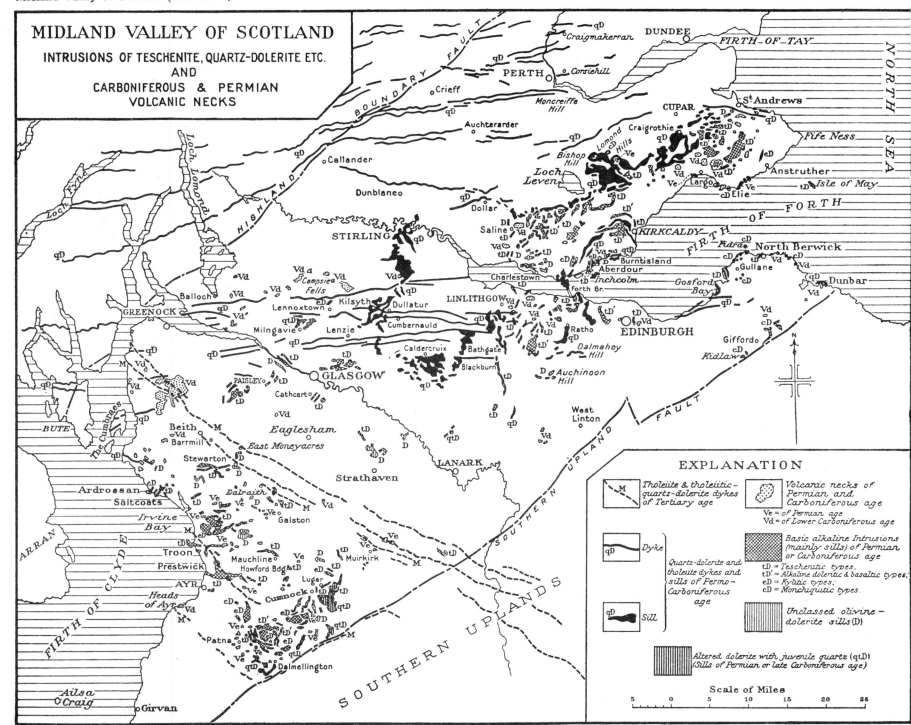

MIDLAND VALLEY OF SCOTLAND

INTRUSIONS OF TESCHENITE, QUARTZ-DOLERITE ETC.
AND
CARBONIFEROUS & PERMIAN
VOLCANIC NECKS

EXPLANATION

M — Tholeiite & tholeiitic-quartz-dolerite dykes of Tertiary age	Volcanic necks of Permian and Carboniferous age
	Ve = of Permian age
	Vd = of Lower Carboniferous age
qD — Dyke	Basic alkaline Intrusions (mainly sills) of Permian or Carboniferous age
	tD = Teschenitic types.
Quartz-dolerite and tholeiite dykes and sills of Permo-Carboniferous age	tD' = Alkaline doleritic & basaltic types;
	eD = Kylitic types;
	cD = Monchiquitic types.
qD — Sill	Unclassed olivine-dolerite sills (D)
	Altered dolerite with juvenile quartz (qtD) (Sills of Permian or late Carboniferous age)

Scale of Miles

5   0   5   10   15   20   25

(For explanation, *see* p. vii.)

CHARACTERISTIC FEATURES OF BASIC ALKALINE INTRUSIONS AND OF ASSOCIATED DOLERITIC SILLS

ROCK GROUPS	GENERAL REMARKS	ROCK NAMES	CHARACTERISTIC MINERALS
KYLITIC TYPES	Usually rich in olivine (often between 10 per cent and 40 per cent); usually nepheline-bearing (up to 7 per cent or more); analcite usually turbid, and less abundant than in teschenitic types (often 5 per cent or less); purplish augite, especially in finer-grained types, frequently forms clusters (polysomatic groups), sometimes along with olivine; augites, when large, have almost colourless centres and reddish-purple rims. Biotite may occur as an accessory mineral.	Essexite.	Plagioclase feldspar, augite, olivine, alkali feldspar, analcite, iron-ore, apatite.
		Theralitic essexite.	As in essexite, with the addition of nepheline.
		Theralite and olivine-rich theralite (=kylite), basanite.	Olivine, augite, plagioclase feldspar, nepheline, analcite, iron-ore, apatite.
		Picrite.	Olivine, augite, a little plagioclase feldspar, iron-ore, apatite.
TESCHENITIC TYPES	Normal rocks contain less olivine than typical kylitic types (often 5 per cent to 15 per cent); usually without nepheline, and rich in analcite (often about 15 per cent); some types contain much brown hornblende (barkevikite) or red-brown biotite; augite pale-brownish to purple; finer-grained ('basaltic') types texturally resemble finer-grained kylites.	Teschenite, hornblende - teschenite, camptonite, nepheline-teschenite.	Plagioclase feldspar, augite, olivine, analcite, iron-ore, apatite, (hornblende, biotite, nepheline).
		Picrite, hornblende-picrite.	Olivine, augite, a little plagioclase feldspar, iron-ore, apatite, (hornblende, biotite, analcite).
		Bekinkinite.	Olivine, augite, hornblende, plagioclase feldspar, alkali feldspar, nepheline, analcite, iron-ore, apatite.
		Hornblende-peridotite.	Olivine, augite, hornblende, iron-ore, biotite.
MONCHIQUITIC TYPES	Very fine-grained; often contain many xenoliths of sedimentary rocks or of olivine-pyroxenite or peridotite, and large xenocrysts of hornblende, augite, biotite, alkali feldspar, etc.; large apatite crystals are also very characteristic.	Monchiquite, nepheline - monchiquite (='nepheline-basalt').	Olivine, augite, analcite, iron-ore, apatite (nepheline).
		Analcite - basanite (=monchiquitic basalt).	Olivine, augite, analcite, plagioclase feldspar, iron-ore, apatite.
		Nepheline-basanite, leucite-basanite.	Olivine, augite, analcite, nepheline or leucite, plagioclase feldspar, iron-ore, apatite.
DOLERITIC and BASALTIC TYPES	Essentially olivine-dolerites or basalts without nepheline, but with a little analcite; may be ophitic sub-ophitic, or intergranular.	Olivine-dolerite, olivine-basalt.	Plagioclase feldspar, augite, olivine, iron-ore, apatite, (analcite).
ALTERED DOLERITIC TYPES	Dolerites containing much chlorite or serpentine, and with olivine and/or augite largely or completely decomposed; alteration is due to deuteric (juvenile or late-magmatic) agencies.	Chloritized olivine-dolerite with residual analcite. *[Some sills of this type contain a picrite layer.]*	As in olivine-dolerite, with decomposition products such as chlorite and calcite.
		Chloritized olivine-dolerite with juvenile quartz. *[Rock of this type occurs in a sill-complex along with teschenite and picrite.]*	As in olivine-dolerite, with much chlorite, calcite, etc., and some quartz or micropegmatite.
		Chloritized olivine-free dolerite with traces of quartz.	Plagioclase feldspar, augite, iron-ore, with much chlorite, calcite, etc., and traces of quartz.

Note. Other zeolites may occur along with, or instead of, analcite.

F

In the east of Scotland kylitic types have been recognized only in Fife, where intrusions resembling the finer-grained varieties of the Ayrshire sills occur at Obelisk Hill in Aberdour, Dunikier (Dunicher) Law, Spalefield and Kingask (*cf.* MacGregor, 1930, Ayrshire, p. 274).

Teschenitic Types form numerous sills both in the east and west of Central Scotland. Among the better known occurrences north of the Firth of Forth are those of Lathones, Crossgates, Radernie and Craighall in East Fife, and those at Braefoot Point (Aberdour) and near Charlestown in West Fife. The island of Inchcolm in the Firth of Forth is mainly a composite teschenitic sill, while further east the Isle of May is also formed of teschenite.

On the south of the Firth, the more important occurrences are the Gullane, Gosford Bay, Salisbury Craigs (Plate IIIB), Mons Hill-Whitehouse Point, Craigie, and Blackburn sills.

In the Glasgow and Paisley districts several teschenite sills occur. The Shettleston sills in particular form an important source of road-metal and setts.

Along the northern border of the Ayrshire Coalfield there are teschenite sills in the neighbourhood of Ardrossan, Stewarton and Galston, while others occur further south and west (*e.g.* Cumnock and Lugar). 'Crinanite' sills are found in Ayrshire near Troon, Prestwick, Mauchline and Howford Bridge.

The teschenitic sills (excluding 'crinanitic' types) vary in grain-size, in texture and in the proportion of their constituent minerals. Nepheline is only occasionally present. Alkaline felsic 'segregation' veins are not uncommonly found in both teschenites and crinanites. The coarser types of teschenite may be ophitic or non-ophitic and sometimes appear to form bands or schlieren. Little detailed study of these variations has been carried out except in those sills containing a layer of basic rock (picroteschenite,[1] picrite,[2] or picrite and perido-tite).[3] The ultrabasic layer (50 to 80 ft.) usually lies wholly or mainly below the centre of the sill[4] of which the total thickness varies from about 140 to 280 ft. Above the picritic layer is a thick layer of variable, sometimes banded, teschenite, and below is a similar but much thinner teschenite layer. The picritic layer may become more basic and olivine-rich downwards (*e.g.* Lugar), but this is not always the case and it may even contain one or more teschenitic bands. Picrite or teschenite may be cut by late alkaline felsic veins and sometimes by still later fine-grained, chilled, basic veins.

Various theories have been put forward to explain the formation of particular examples of the banded teschenitic sills: these include (1) intrusion of a hetero-geneous magma with immiscible liquid layer (Grabham, 1910); (2) successive

[1] Braefoot.
[2] The surface outcrops of Inchcolm, Blackburn and Craigens (Cumnock), and occurrences proved underground in mineral borings at Easter Dalmeny, Blackness and Saline.
[3] Lugar and Ardrossan (hornblende-peridotite).
[4] In one abnormal sill-complex at Craigens (Cumnock) picrite is found at the top (MacGregor, 1949).

injections of teschenitic magma, with gravitative differentiation *in situ* in the latest (median) layer (*e.g.* Tyrrell, 1917); (3) Concentration of olivine in the magma-reservoir before or during intrusion, and injection of olivine-enriched magma at a late stage (Bailey and Bowen, 1928; Flett, 1931).

Camptonitic teschenite rich in brown hornblende is not uncommon as a local facies in the teschenitic sills. The occurrence of camptonite as separate intrusions is very rare, one of the few examples being a small sill at Craigie in Ayrshire (MacGregor, 1930). A few north-west camptonite dykes of uncertain age are known in North Ayrshire and Lanarkshire.

Bekinkinite is a nepheline-bearing basic facies of the teschenitic magma, found in a sill at Barshaw near Paisley, and as part of a composite plug at Carskeoch Hill near Patna (Tyrrell, 1928; MacGregor, 1949).

Few teschenite dykes are known[1] and the only intrusion of plug-like form is that of Carskeoch Hill.

Monchiquitic Types. These intrusions are abundant both in the east and in the west of the Midland Valley. In Fife, monchiquites, analcite-basanites and nepheline-basanites occur as intrusions (often dykes) in volcanic necks, some of which are of Lower Carboniferous age. An extensive nepheline-basanite sill is also known (Fordell Castle). The vent-intrusions often enclose large crystals (usually corroded or broken xenocrysts) of brown hornblende, augite, biotite, soda-rich alkali feldspar (anorthoclase or soda-microcline) and garnet (pyrope) known locally as the 'Elie ruby.' Zircon has also been recorded. Nodules composed of olivine (replaced by serpentine, talc and carbonates) and brown chrome-spinel, of brown hornblende, biotite and feldspar, or of brown hornblende, biotite and green chrome-diopside are also common as enclosures in the intrusions (Wallace, 1916; Balsillie, 1927, 1927a). The above-mentioned minerals and nodules often occur also in the tuffs of the necks, and it has been pointed out that the assemblage recalls the xenocrystic content of the 'blue ground' of the South African diamond pipes.

A similar assemblage of xenocrysts and nodules characterizes many of the monchiquitic rocks that form small intrusions in and near the Permian necks of Central Ayrshire; garnet and zircon have, however, not been recorded, but large apatites are found. Nepheline-basanite intrusions and carbonated peridotite nodules occur in one Ayrshire vent of Calciferous Sandstone age, that of the Heads of Ayr (Eyles, 1929). Near the Permian necks xenocrystic monchiquites form dykes or sills a few feet in thickness. In Ayrshire, dykes of monchiquite with an E.–W. or W.N.W. trend are common in the Coal Measures of the Irvine Valley area and in the Limestone Coal Group of the Patna district. Some of

---

[1] Many 'crinanite' dykes with a N.W. or N.N.W. trend occur in Ayrshire, but there is good reason (p. 82) for regarding them as being of Tertiary age. A few analcite-poor crinanite dykes that run in other directions may be Permian (MacGregor, 1930).

these, like certain of the Permian vent-intrusions, are full of small sedimentary xenoliths. A few monchiquite dykes cut post-Coal Measures teschenitic sills in Ayrshire.

In East Lothian numerous intrusions of monchiquitic types, including analcite and nepheline-basanites, and leucite-basanite recently found by Mr. Balsillie, occur as vent-intrusions, stocks and sills. Some of these East Lothian rocks contain peridotite or pyroxenite nodules.

Doleritic and Basaltic Types are scarce except in Fife where they are well developed as large sills, for instance at Balcarres, Kilbrackmont and Baldutho (intergranular basaltic types), Gilston and Drumcarrow (sub-ophitic doleritic types), Gathercauld, Greigston and Wilkieston (ophitic doleritic types), Raith and Galliston (porphyritic types).

Altered Doleritic Types. Most of these sills are olivine-bearing. Sills of olivine-dolerite in which chlorite is abundant replacing olivine and analcite, and in which even augite is not always preserved, are found in Ayrshire near Dalmellington (Corbie Craigs sill), in Midlothian at Corstorphine Hill, and in West Lothian south of Uphall (Houston Wood or Stankards sill). The latter occurrence has been proved by boring to be about 217 ft. thick; in it is a 123-ft. layer of picrite, the thickest mass of ultrabasic rock known in any Scottish sill; olivine is fresh only in the centre of the picrite band. A picrite layer also occurs in the Corstorphine sill near Barnton, where it is cut by pale feldspathic veins rich in zeolites. The chloritized doleritic portion of the Stankards sill is rather similar to the altered dolerite sill of Auchinoon (Midlothian) which, however, contains abundant chlorophaeite (Campbell and Lunn, 1927).

Highly decomposed olivine-dolerite with juvenile quartz ('quartz de corrosion') forms extensive sill-outcrops in Ayrshire near Dalmellington and Cumnock. These rocks are very different from the normal quartz-dolerites of the Midland Valley, but form a connecting link between the latter and the doleritic intrusions of teschenitic affinities. At Cumnock (Craigens–Avisyard sill-complex) the altered quartz-bearing dolerite is associated with teschenitic types, including picrite (MacGregor, 1949).

Other highly decomposed dolerites form sills at Burntisland in Fife and at Milngavie north of Glasgow; no olivine has been detected in them and they contain minute and very sporadic patches of quartz.

Age of the Intrusions. In the west of the Midland Valley, particularly in Ayrshire, many of the sills cut Coal Measures, and there is little doubt that in this district the suite as a whole is genetically connected with the Permian volcanic period. (Possible exceptions include the so-called 'crinanite' sills, some of which cut Permian lavas or sediments and may be of Tertiary age, the alkaline dolerite sill of Craigie, Ayrshire, petrographically similar to Millstone Grit lavas, and the monchiquitic intrusions in the Lower Carboniferous neck of the Heads of

Ayr). Many of the intrusions may be older than the Permian lavas, for blocks of kylitic and teschenitic type have been found in certain of the Permian agglomerate vents, and certain kylitic and teschenitic sills are pierced by Permian necks, or cut by monchiquitic dykes similar to intrusions associated with these necks.

In Fife and the Lothians the intrusions cut sediments which are mainly of Calciferous Sandstone and Carboniferous Limestone age, but are absent from the Coal Measures; it has therefore usually been assumed that they are genetically connected with the Lower Carboniferous volcanoes and were injected in Lower Carboniferous times. In support of this hypothesis, no really satisfactory evidence has ever been adduced.

In East Lothian, however, veins of sediment of Calciferous Sandstone facies (sandstone, mudstone or cementstone) have been recorded in a monchiquite sill,[1] a teschenite sill, a volcanic neck, and lava-flows.[2] The writer has recently noticed similar veins in bedded tuffs of Calciferous Sandstone age, and in associated volcanic vents, on the coast east of North Berwick. In Fife, sandstone veins, ascribed to the infilling of earthquake fissures by unconsolidated sand, have been recorded in the Braefoot teschenite sill. All these igneous rocks are found among Calciferous Sandstone sediments.

Whatever be the exact origin of the sedimentary veins, their presence implies that the igneous rocks that they traverse cannot be younger than the Calciferous Sandstone period. Here, then, is definite evidence that some at least of the eastern teschenites and monchiquites are of Lower Carboniferous age.

Teschenitic sills are cut by E.–W. quartz-dolerite dykes on Inchcolm and at Wester Ochiltree near Linlithgow (p. 75).

SELECTED REFERENCES

General.

1923. TYRRELL, G. W., Classification and Age of the Analcite-bearing Igneous Rocks of Scotland, *Geol. Mag.*, pp. 249–260.

1923. WALKER, F., Notes on the Classification of Scottish and Moravian Teschenites, *Geol. Mag.*, pp. 242–249.

1928. BAILEY, E. B., quoted by N. L. Bowen, in The Evolution of the Igneous Rocks (Princeton Univ. Press), pp. 173, 174.

1929. EYLES, V. A., J. B. SIMPSON and A. G. MACGREGOR, The Igneous Geology of Central Ayrshire, *Trans. Geol. Soc. Glasgow*, vol. xviii, part iii, pp. 374–387.

1931. GUPPY, E. M., and H. H. THOMAS, Chemical Analyses of Igneous Rocks, Metamorphic Rocks, and Minerals (*Mem. Geol. Surv.*), pp. 67, 75, 87, 89–96.

1934. WALKER, F., The Term 'Crinanite', *Geol. Mag.*, pp. 122–128.

1937. TOMKEIEFF, S. I., Petrochemistry of the Scottish Carboniferous-Permian Igneous Rocks, *Bull. Volcanol.*, Sér. ii, tome i, pp. 59–87.

---

[1] T. C. Day, *Trans. Edin. Geol. Soc.*, vol. xi, part iii, 1925, pp. 306, 307.

[2] T. C. Day, *op. cit.* vol. x, part ii, 1914, pp. 114–119; and 'The Geology of East Lothian' (*Mem. Geol. Surv.*), 1910, pp. 75–79, 91–101.

Fife and the Lothians.

1908. CAMPBELL, R., and A. G. STENHOUSE, The Geology of Inchcolm, *Trans. Edin. Geol. Soc.*, vol. ix, part ii, pp. 121–134 (Read 1907).

1910. FLETT, J. S., and G. W. GRABHAM, in The Geology of the Neighbourhood of Edinburgh (*Mem. Geol. Surv.*), pp. 281, 289–301.

1910. BAILEY, E. B., in The Geology of East Lothian (*Mem. Geol. Surv.*), pp. 105–117.

1916. WALLACE, Mrs., Notes on the Petrology of the Agglomerates and Hypabyssal Intrusions between Largo and St. Monans, *Trans. Edin. Geol. Soc.*, vol. x, part iii, pp. 348–361.

1922. BALSILLIE, D., Notes on the Dolerite Intrusions of East Fife, *Geol. Mag.*, pp. 442–452.

1923. WALKER, F., The Igneous Geology of the Dalmeny District, *Trans. Roy. Soc. Edin.*, vol. liii, part ii, pp. 361–375.

1924. ALLAN, D. A., The Igneous Geology of the Burntisland District, *Trans. Roy. Soc. Edin.*, vol. liii, part iii, pp. 479–501.

1926. WALKER, F., The Teschenite Sill of Charlestown, Fife, *Geol. Mag.*, pp. 343–347.

1927. BALSILLIE, D., East Fife Igneous Geology, *Proc. Geol. Assoc.*, vol. xxxviii, pp. 463–469.

1927a. BALSILLIE, D., Contemporaneous Volcanic Activity in East Fife, *Geol. Mag.*, pp. 489–91.

1927. CAMPBELL, R., and J. W. LUNN, The Tholeiites and Dolerites of the Dalmahoy Syncline, *Trans. Roy. Soc. Edin.*, vol. lv, part ii, pp. 489–505.

1928. WALKER, F. and J. IRVING, The Igneous Intrusions between St. Andrews and Loch Leven, *Trans. Roy. Soc. Edin.*, vol. lvi, part i, pp. 1–17.

1928. SIMPSON, J. B., Notes on the Geology of the Kidlaw District, East Lothian, *Trans. Edin. Geol. Soc.*, vol. xii, part i, pp. 111–113.

1930. FLETT, Sir J. S., The Teschenite of Easter Dalmeny, in Summary of Progress for 1929, Part III (*Mem. Geol. Surv.*), pp. 59–74.

1931. FLETT, Sir J. S., The Saline No. 1 Teschenite, in Summary of Progress for 1930, Part II (*Mem. Geol. Surv.*), pp. 44–50.

1931. FLETT, Sir J. S., The Blackness Teschenite, in Summary of Progress for 1930, Part III (*Mem. Geol. Surv.*), pp. 39–45.

1931. ALLAN, D. A., A Nepheline Basanite Sill at Fordell, Fife, *Proc. Liverpool Geol. Soc.*, vol. xv, part iv, pp. 309–317.

1932. FLETT, Sir J. S., The Stankards Sill, in Summary of Progress for 1931, Part II (*Mem. Geol. Surv.*), pp. 141–155.

1932. CAMPBELL, R., T. C. DAY and A. G. STENHOUSE, The Braefoot Outer Sill, Fife: Part I, *Trans. Edin. Geol. Soc.*, vol. xii, part iv, pp. 342–375.

1934. CAMPBELL, R., T. C. DAY and A. G. STENHOUSE, The Braefoot Outer Sill, Fife: Part II, *Trans. Edin. Geol. Soc.*, vol. xiii, part i, pp. 148–173.

1936. BALSILLIE, D., Leucite-Basanite in East Lothian, *Geol. Mag.*, pp. 16–19.

1936. WALKER, F., Geology of the Isle of May, *Trans. Edin. Geol. Soc.*, vol. xiii, part iii, pp. 275–285.

Glasgow District and Ayrshire.

1911. BAILEY, E. B., in The Geology of the Glasgow District (*Mem. Geol. Surv.*), pp. 128–135; 2nd Edition, 1925, pp. 164–175.

1912. TYRRELL, G. W., The Late Palaeozoic Alkaline Igneous Rocks of the West of Scotland, *Geol. Mag.*, pp. 69–80, 120–131.

1915. TYRRELL, G. W., The Bekinkinite of Barshaw, *Geol. Mag.*, pp. 304–311, 361–366.

1917. TYRRELL, G. W., The Picrite-Teschenite Sill of Lugar (Ayrshire), *Quart. Journ. Geol. Soc.*, vol. lxxii, pp. 84–131.

1923. TYRRELL, G. W., Classification and Age of the Analcite-bearing Igneous Rocks of Scotland, *Geol. Mag.*, pp. 249–260.

1928a. TYRRELL, G. W., On some Dolerite-Sills containing Analcite-Syenite in Central Ayrshire, *Quart. Journ. Geol. Soc.*, vol. lxxxiv, pp. 540–569.

1928b. TYRRELL, G. W., A Further Contribution to the Petrography of the Late-Palaeozoic Igneous Suite of the West of Scotland, *Trans. Geol. Soc. Glasgow*, vol. xviii, part ii, pp. 259–294.

1929. EYLES, V. A., and others, The Igneous Geology of Central Ayrshire, *Trans. Geol. Soc. Glasgow*, vol. xviii, part iii, pp. 374–387.

1930. MACGREGOR, A. G., in The Geology of North Ayrshire (*Mem. Geol. Surv.*), pp. 265–278.

1932. SIMPSON, J. B., and A. G. MACGREGOR, Economic Geology of the Ayrshire Coalfields, Area IV (*Mem. Geol. Surv.*), p. 128, etc.

1945. PATTERSON, E. M., The Distribution of trace-elements in a Scottish Permo-Carboniferous Teschenite and its Lugaritic differentiate, *Geol. Mag.*, pp. 230–234.

1946. PATTERSON, E. M., The Teschenite–Picrite Sill of Saltcoats, Ayrshire, *Trans. Geol. Soc. Glasgow*, vol. xxi, part i, pp. 1–28.

1949. MACGREGOR, A. G., and others in The Geology of Central Ayrshire (*Mem. Geol. Surv.*), Chapters X–XII.

VII. THE QUARTZ-DOLERITE AND THOLEIITE DYKES AND SILLS OF PERMO-CARBONIFEROUS AGE

A STRIKING feature of the geology of Central Scotland is the presence of broad quartz-dolerite dykes, with a general E.–W. trend, which have been traced for long distances (Plate VI). They cut rocks ranging from Lower Old Red Sandstone to Coal Measures. Thick sills of quartz-dolerite are also prominent in the Carboniferous sediments (including Coal Measures) in the counties of Fife, Stirling, Lanark, West Lothian and Midlothian, and have long been regarded as genetically connected with the dykes.

Dykes. Many of the dykes can be traced more or less continuously in the Midland Valley for distances of ten to fifty miles. The longest are (1) the Campsie dyke which stretches from the Firth of Forth to the Firth of Clyde, and (2) a dyke passing just south of Perth which extends from Fifeshire to Glen Artney. Westwards across the Highland schists, where they are accompanied by many less continuous dykes, these two intrusions have been traced as far as the neighbourhood of Loch Fyne; their maximum known length is thus about eighty miles. The majority of the long dykes range in breadth from 60 ft. to about 150 ft.

In the Midland Valley the dykes traverse sediments and lavas of Old Red Sandstone and Carboniferous age. The trend of most of the dykes in the Highland schists, and of the few examples in the Old Red Sandstone north of the latitude of Arbroath, is somewhat south of west. The local south-westerly deflection of the Perth dykes near the Highland Boundary Fault between Crieff and Callander may be compared with the deflection of big Tertiary dykes near the Southern Upland Fault (p. 81).

The most southerly representative of the big quartz-dolerite dykes lies four miles north-west of Ardrossan. Tholeiites (see below) which may belong to the Permo-Carboniferous suite are, however, represented among the numerous narrower (10 ft. to 20 ft.) dykes proved during mining operations in the Coal Measures of the Irvine Valley (MacGregor, 1930).

Petrographically the majority of the dykes are quartz-dolerites composed of basic plagioclase feldspar, augite and rhombic pyroxene (hypersthene), with interstitial micropegmatite or quartz and cryptocrystalline mesostasis, apatite and iron-ore. Pyrites is often abundant and hornblende sometimes fringes the augite. Rocks without micropegmatite, but containing a mesostasis of more or less devitrified brownish glass, and sometimes pseudomorphs which may represent olivine, have been called tholeiites (e.g. in Perthshire). Serpentinous pseudomorphs after olivine sometimes occur in fine-grained tholeiitic marginal portions of the quartz-dolerite dykes. Quartzo-feldspathic segregation veins are usually found in the normal quartz-dolerites. Attention has recently been drawn to the occurrence, in dykes and sills, of late basaltic veins of similar composition to the normal rock (Walker, 1935).

An exceptional glassy rock rich in chlorophaeite (tholeiite of Bankhead type; Walker, 1930) occurs in a broad dyke-exposure north-west of Kinkell near Lennoxtown.

The quartz-dolerite and tholeiite dykes have been widely exploited for use in road-making.

Sills. The quartz-dolerite sills often form prominent hills or scarp features. The most notable example of the latter is the bold crag on which Stirling Castle stands, part of a sill which extends southwards for eight miles. The neighbouring Abbey Craig (Plate IIIA) is a portion of the same intrusion. In Fife quartz-dolerite sheets form high ground near the Lomond Hills (e.g. Bishop Hill and White Craigs), and at Walton and Clatto Hills, Benarty and Dumglow. Similar rock at North Queensferry supports the northern and central parts of the Forth Bridges. South of the Firth smaller outcrops occur at Hound Point, West Craigs, and Ratho, and in the Bathgate Hills at Kettlestoun and Carribber. Important outcrops also occur in the Central Coalfield near Blackridge, Caldercruix and Kilsyth.

In thickness the more important sills vary from 80 ft. or less up to about 300 ft. Mineralogically they are similar to the normal quartz-dolerite dykes. In the Kilsyth district and elsewhere (e.g. Stirling, Ratho) sills show a fairly consistent variation in facies from top to bottom (Robertson, 1937). In the upper

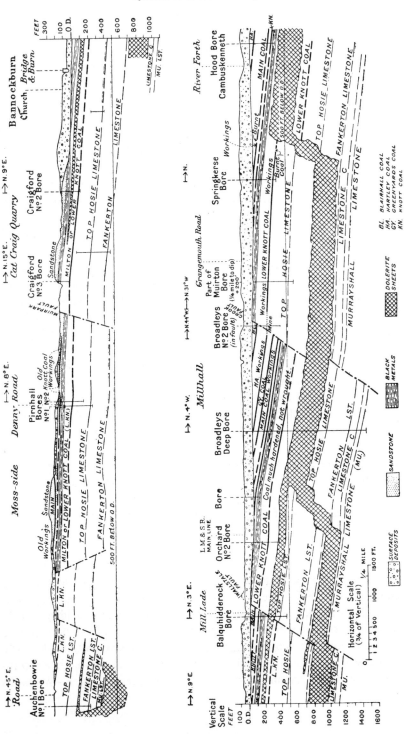

FIG. 15. *Section across Carboniferous Limestone Series near Stirling, to illustrate the behaviour of the Stirling quartz-dolerite sill*

third part of the thickness of the sill a relatively thin and fine-grained zone at the top is succeeded downwards by a much thicker and very coarse-grained zone; the lower two-thirds consist of medium-grained (normal) quartz-dolerite such as characterizes many of the E.–W. dykes. Vertical and horizontal quartzo-feldspathic 'segregation' veins are common, as has long been recognized.

A very fine-grained sill that probably represents a rapidly cooled intrusion of quartz-dolerite magma occurs at Binny Craig in West Lothian. This well-known rock has been called a basalt of Binny Craig type. It contains small phenocrysts of feldspar and augite but is mineralogically and chemically similar to a quartz-dolerite.

A sill of tholeiite (Bankhead type; Walker, 1930) occurring near Dalmeny Station, West Lothian, closely resembles the glassy tholeiitic portion of the Kinkell dyke (above).

A unique type of tholeiite is found in the neighbourhood of Dalmahoy Hill, south-west of Edinburgh. The main outcrop is a composite olivine-bearing sill, with doleritic, basaltic and tholeiitic (glassy) portions, in all of which chlorophaeite occurs abundantly as a replacement product after olivine (fayalite) and as an interstitial mineral. Apart from the presence of olivine the glassy portion of the sill (tholeiite of Dalmahoy Type) at once recalls the tholeiites of Bankhead type mentioned above. The writer regards the intrusion as most probably an abnormal member of the Permo-Carboniferous quartz-dolerite suite. Campbell and Lunn consider it to be a Lower Carboniferous intrusive equivalent of mugearite lava. No such intrusions, however, accompany the numerous mugearite lavas found elsewhere in the Midland Valley.

The larger quartz-dolerite and tholeiite sills are extensively quarried as sources of road-metal, paving setts or kerb stones.

Age of Dykes and Sills. Apart from petrographical similarity, other evidence connecting the dykes with the sills has been obtained. The Lenzie-Torphichen dyke, extending for more than twenty-five miles from Glasgow to the Bathgate Hills, has acted as a feeder for sills at different horizons in the Carboniferous sediments, at Mollinburn and near Torphichen. There is very strong circumstantial evidence that the Dullatur and Cumbernauld dykes are the feeders of sills at Kilsyth. Again, the quartz-dolerite intrusion along the pre-existing E.–W. Ochil Fault near Dollar (Clackmannanshire) is regarded as a steeply inclined sheet which connected quartz-dolerite sills at different stratigraphical levels on opposite sides of the dislocation, near Stirling and in Fife (Dinham and Haldane, 1932).

Quartz-dolerite sills at different stratigraphical horizons have been proved in mining operations to be connected by steeply transgressive portions (Fig. 15), for example near Stirling and Kilsyth. In other instances sills attain higher stratigraphical horizons by passing horizontally across pre-existing E.–W. faults (Fig. 15).

These quartz-dolerite intrusions of the Midland Valley are thus products of *one phase* of post-Coal Measures magmatic intrusion. That the period of intrusion was somewhat prolonged is indicated by a variety of evidence. A case is known, for instance, where a very thin portion of a sill cuts a dyke (near Ravencraig; Bailey, 1910). Again, although, as we have seen, some sills and dykes are later than E.–W. faults, others appear to have been affected by faults with the same trend (*e.g.* the Ravencraig sill). This E.–W. faulting is believed to be connected with Permo-Carboniferous earth-movements, which affected the Carboniferous strata before, and possibly after, the Scottish Permian rocks were deposited. The intrusion of quartz-dolerite magma thus probably took place during the Permo-Carboniferous earth-movements. In two instances in the east of Scotland teschenitic sills are cut by E.–W. quartz-dolerite dykes; the quartz-dolerites are therefore younger than some, if not all, of the teschenitic sills (p. 69).

Fife has supplied evidence helping to set an upper age limit. The volcanic vents of the Lomond Hills pierce a quartz-dolerite sill (Walker and Irving, 1928), and fragments of quartz-dolerite of similar type (Walker, 1935) have been found in certain agglomerate necks near Elie. As these volcanic orifices can only be of Permian age (p. 78) and are presumably roughly contemporaneous with the Mauchline lavas, it is probable that the quartz-dolerites were intruded in late Carboniferous times or early in the Permian period before the outpouring of the basal lavas that rest on eroded Carboniferous strata in the Mauchline basin. A less precise upper age limit has long been recognized, for in West Renfrewshire (*e.g.* at Inverkip) and across the Firth of Clyde in Bute and in the Highland Schists of Cowal, E.–W. quartz-dolerite dykes are cut by N.W. Tertiary dykes.

Petrographically the quartz-dolerite suite of the Midland Valley, although typically much coarser in grain, is otherwise similar to the Whin sill and related dykes of Northern England and has long been regarded ·as contemporaneous with them. These intrusions cut Coal Measures and are older than the Upper Brockram and Yellow Sands of the Permian. The general agreement with the Scottish evidence is thus very striking.

SELECTED REFERENCES

General.
1935. WALKER, F., The late Palaeozoic quartz-dolerites and tholeiites of Scotland, *Mineralogical Mag.*, vol. xxiv, pp. 131–159. (Comprehensive account of geology and petrology; collected analyses.)
1937. TOMKEIEFF, S. I., Petrochemistry of the Scottish Carboniferous–Permian Igneous Rocks, *Bull. Volcanol.*, Sér ii., tome i, pp. 59–87.

Perthshire.
1908. MACNAIR, PETER, *The Geology and Scenery of the Grampians and the Valley of Strathmore* (Maclehose & Sons, Glasgow), vol. ii, pp. 83–101 (Numerous photographs).

1934. WALKER, F., A Preliminary Account of the Quartz-dolerite Dykes of Perthshire. *Trans. and Proc. Perthshire Soc. of Nat. Sci.*, vol. ix, part iv, pp. 109–117.

Fife.

1928. WALKER, F., and J. IRVING, The Igeneous Intrusions between St. Andrews and Loch Leven, *Trans. Roy. Soc. Edin.*, vol. lvi, part i, pp. 1–17.
1942. PHEMISTER, J., and A. G. MACGREGOR, Datolite, etc., in a contact-altered limestone at Chapel Quarry, Fife, *Mineralogical Mag.*, vol. xxvi, pp. 275–282.

Clackmannanshire, Stirlingshire, Lanarkshire and Dumbartonshire.

1909. TYRRELL, G. W., The Geology and Petrology of the Intrusions of the Kilsyth-Croy District, Dumbartonshire, *Geol. Mag.*, pp. 299–309, 359–366.
1925. BAILEY, E. B., C. H. DINHAM and C. B. CRAMPTON, in The Geology of the Glasgow District (*Mem. Geol. Surv.*), 2nd Edition, pp. 149–151, 192–198.
1927. DINHAM, C. H., Stirling District, *Proc. Geol. Assoc.*, vol. xxxviii, pp. 476–481.
1930. WALKER, F., A tholeiitic phase of the quartz-dolerite magma of Central Scotland, *Mineralogical Mag.*, vol. xxii, pp. 368–376.
1932. DINHAM, C. H., and D. HALDANE, The Economic Geology of the Stirling and Clackmannan Coalfield (*Mem. Geol. Surv.*), pp. 170–173, 181–192.
1937. ROBERTSON, T., in The Economic Geology of the Central Coalfield: Area I, Kilsyth and Kirkintilloch (*Mem. Geol. Surv.*), pp. 102–105.
1942. ANDERSON, E. M., *The Dynamics of Faulting and Dyke Formation with Applications to Britain* (Oliver and Boyd, Edinburgh), pp. 29–36, 48–53, 167–183; 2nd Edition, 1951, pp. 31–39, 52–58, 179–199.
1952. WALKER, F., Differentiation in a Quartz-dolerite sill at Northfield Quarry, Stirlingshire, *Trans. Edin. Geol. Soc.*, vol. xv, pp. 393–405.
1952. WALKER, F., H. C. G. VINCENT and R. L. MITCHELL, The Chemistry and Mineralogy of the Kinkell Tholeiite, Stirlingshire, *Mineralogical Mag.*, vol. xxix, pp. 895–908.

The Lothians.

1906. FALCONER, J. D., The Igneous Geology of the Bathgate and Linlithgow Hills, *Trans. Roy. Soc. Edin.*, vol. xlv, part i, pp. 137–149.
1910. FLETT, J. S., E. B. BAILEY and others, in The Geology of the Neighbourhood of Edinburgh (*Mem. Geol. Surv.*), 2nd Edition, pp. 282–286, 301–308.
1923. WALKER, F., The Igneous Geology of the Dalmeny District, *Trans. Roy. Soc. Edin.*, vol. liii, part ii, pp. 365–366, 374.
1927. CAMPBELL, R., and J. W. LUNN, The Tholeiites and Dolerites of the Dalmahoy Syncline, *Trans. Roy. Soc. Edin.*, vol. lv, part ii, pp. 489–505.
1928. LUNN, J. W., The Intrusion of Binny Craig, West Lothian, *Trans. Edin. Geol. Soc.*, vol. xii, part i, pp. 74–79.

Ayrshire and Buteshire.

1916. SMELLIE, W. R., The Igneous Rocks of Bute, *Trans. Geol. Soc. Glasgow*, vol. xv, part iii, pp. 363–364.
1917. TYRRELL, G. W., The Igneous Geology of the Cumbrae Islands, Firth of Clyde, *Trans. Geol. Soc. Glasgow*, vol. xvi, part ii, pp. 257–258, 267–268.
1930. MACGREGOR, A. G., and others in The Geology of North Ayrshire (*Mem. Geol. Surv.*), pp. 295–298.

A. Dune-bedding in desert sandstone of Permian age, Ballochmyle Quarries, Mauchline, Ayrshire

B. Duncryne, Gartocharn, Dunbartonshire, from the south-west

(For explanation, *see* p. vii.)

VIII. PERMIAN

ROCKS of Permian age cover an oval area, about 30 square miles in extent, in Central Ayrshire, where they have been folded along with underlying Coal Measures to form the Mauchline Basin. They fall into two distinct subdivisions, a lower volcanic group with a maximum thickness of about 500 ft., and an upper sandstone group (the Mauchline Sandstone) which is probably at least 1,500 ft. thick in the centre of the basin.

Permian Sandstone. The Mauchline Sandstone is bright brick-red to orange-red in colour. False-bedding is very pronounced, and the desert origin of the deposit is proved not only by the magnificent large-scale dune-bedding so well displayed in the Ballochmyle Quarries at Mauchline (Plate VIIA) but by the wind-rounding and polishing of the constituent quartz grains. Wind-rounding is shown particularly well in the layers of coarser sand. Red desert sandstone is intimately associated with lava flows and tuffs and locally intervenes between the base of the volcanic sequence and the underlying Carboniferous.

The Mauchline Sandstone has long been quarried and widely used as a building stone in Great Britain and Ireland; it has been even exported to America.

In spite of the lack of fossils there seems no reason to doubt (1) correlation with the desert sandstones and lavas of the Thornhill Basin in Dumfries-shire, (2) the time-equivalence of the Mauchline and Dumfries sandstones with the Penrith Sandstone of the North of England, as advocated for example by Horne and Gregory, or (3) the Permian age of the latter.

Permian Lavas and Volcanic Necks (*Plate VI*). A discussion of the age of the necks of East Fife, about which there is diversity of opinion, is included in this section. Reference has already been made to agglomerates and intrusions in these vents (p. 67).

Lavas. Interbedded volcanic rocks of Permian age occur in the Midland Valley only in Ayrshire, where they consist mainly of lava-flows and form an annular outcrop surrounding the overlying Permian desert sandstones of the Mauchline basin.

The volcanic sequence, about 500 ft. thick, rests unconformably, but with no marked discordance, on the Barren Red Coal Measures.[1] Locally some tuff or desert sandstone intervenes between the Carboniferous and the lava sequence. Tuff with interbedded sandstone separates the lavas from the overlying sandstones near Mauchline and Catrine. Desert sandstone is locally interbedded with

[1] In the Carboniferous outliers at Sanquhar and Thornhill, in the Southern Uplands, Permian lavas rest on lower members of the Carboniferous (Productive Coal Measures).

77

the lava flows; it often penetrates their slaggy tops and is frequently mixed with the igneous fragments of the tuffs.

Microporphyritic olivine-rich basalts (*cf.* Dalmeny type) probably form the majority of the flows, but analcite-and nepheline-basanites and nepheline-monchiquites ('nepheline-basalts') have also been recorded.

Necks. Over sixty volcanic necks which are regarded as connected with the period of eruption of the Mauchline lavas cut the Carboniferous rocks of the Central Ayrshire Coalfield; they lie between Irvine and Galston in the north and Dalmellington and New Cumnock in the south. These necks are correlated with the Permian volcanic episode for the following reasons: (1) three pierce Permian lavas, but none are found in the overlying desert sandstone; (2) forty-six of them cut either Productive or Barren Red Coal Measures; (3) those which cut rocks of Millstone Grit, Carboniferous Limestone or Calciferous Sandstone age (about ten) do so in areas where contemporaneous volcanic products are known to be absent in these strata (Patna district); (4) many of the intrusions or fragments in the necks are either identical with Permian lavas or of closely allied types.

The agglomerates may be composed partly of sedimentary and partly of igneous fragments. The former include pieces of Carboniferous rocks, and occasionally small or large blocks of Permian sandstone. Isolated wind-rounded quartz grains are also very characteristic. The igneous fragments include blocks and lapilli of lava of Permian types, occasional pieces of kylite or teschenite sills, blocks and small nodules of carbonated peridotite, and fragments of large crystals of alkali feldspar (anorthoclase or soda-microcline), augite, hornblende and biotite. The peridotite and crystal fragments are also characteristic of the vent-intrusions, which are predominantly monchiquitic (p. 67), although kylitic and teschenitic types have been found as isolated occurrences (pp. 64, 69).

It may be mentioned here, as having a bearing on the problem of the age of vents in Fife (*below*), that pieces of peridotite and alkali-feldspar have been found in tuff intercalated in sediments of Calciferous Sandstone age at Greenan Castle, near Ayr. The tuff is regarded as contemporaneous with the neighbouring Heads of Ayr vent, in the agglomerate of which occur peridotite fragments and monchiquitic intrusions (Tyrrell, 1920; Eyles, 1949).

A group of vents which are possibly of Permian age pierce Upper Old Red Sandstone and Lower Carboniferous lavas a few miles north of Saltcoats, in north-west Ayrshire. In the extreme east of the county, near Muirkirk, there are seven volcanic necks which may be confidently assigned to the Permian. They cut strata of Silurian and Carboniferous Limestone age in an area where there are no contemporaneous volcanic rocks and they contain wind-rounded quartz-grains. Three of the vents are cut by Tertiary dykes.

There is considerable doubt as to the age or ages of the hundred odd volcanic necks of Eastern Fife, many of which may be seen in section along the coast. They were assigned to the Permian by Sir Archibald Geikie because of their striking petrological resemblance to the Permian necks of Ayrshire (*cf.* pp. 67, 78), because at least one was known to cut Coal Measures, and because, near Largo, he thought bedded tuff connected with one of the necks rested uncomformably on Carboniferous sediments. It has since been shown that Geikie's observations at Largo were faulty, and that tuffs interbedded in the Lower Carboniferous sediments of East Fife are more widespread than he supposed (Balsillie, 1923, 1927). In view of these new observations Mr. Balsillie has advocated a Lower Carboniferous age for many of the teschenite and quartz-dolerite sills of East Fife, and for all the volcanic necks, with the exception of the few that cut Millstone Grit and Coal Measures (Balsillie, 1922, 1923, 1927).

As regards the age of the teschenite sills there is little satisfactory evidence (p. 68). The work of the Geological Survey leaves no reasonable doubt, however, that all the quartz-dolerite sills and dykes belong to one period of intrusion later than the deposition of much, probably all, of the Coal Measures (p. 74). Now two volcanic necks pierce a quartz-dolerite sill in Lower Carboniferous strata near Loch Leven and fragments of quartz-dolerite have been found (p. 75), in the agglomerate of vents near Largo and Elie which, in different instances, cut Coal Measures and Lower Carboniferous rocks (Wallace, 1916; Balsillie, 1923, 1927). It thus seems clear that post-Coal Measures (and therefore Permian) necks do occur in Lower Carboniferous rocks in East Fife. Mr. Balsillie is right, however, in insisting that the remarkable similarity between the vent-intrusions and agglomerates of the East Fife and Ayrshire necks is no proof of the contemporaneity of all these volcanoes. For instance, a vent east of St. Andrews which is cut by a quartz-dolerite dyke is presumably of Lower Carboniferous age. The occurrence of isolated well-rounded quartz-grains in many of the Fife necks,[1] when considered in conjunction with the frequent presence of such grains in the Ayrshire Permian vents near the desert sandstones of Mauchline, would, however, appear to favour a Permian age for those necks in which they are found.

SELECTED REFERENCES

General.
1937. MacGregor, A. G., The Carboniferous and Permian Volcanoes of Scotland, *Bull. Volcanol.*, Sér. ii, tome i, pp. 41–58.

Ayrshire.
1909. Boyle, R., The Economic and Petrographic Geology of the New Red Sandstones of the South and West of Scotland, *Trans. Geol. Soc. Glasgow*, vol. xiii, part iii, pp. 344–384.
1912. Tyrrell, G. W., The Late-Palaeozoic Alkaline Igneous Rocks of the West of Scotland, *Geol. Mag.*, pp. 125–131.
1920. Tyrrell, G. W., The Igneous Geology of the Ayrshire Coast from Doonfoot to the Heads of Ayr, *Trans. Geol. Soc. Glasgow*, vol. xvi, part iii, pp. 339–363.

[1] Geikie, A., 'Geology of Eastern Fife' (*Mem. Geol. Surv.*), 1902, p. 278.

1924. EYLES, V. A., Note on the Nature and Age of Scottish Rocks bearing Xenocrysts of Anorthoclase or Soda-microcline, *Geol. Mag.*, pp. 471–472.

1928. TYRRELL, G. W., A Further Contribution to the Petrography of the Late-Palaeozoic Igneous Suite of the West of Scotland. *Trans. Geol. Soc. Glasgow*, vol. xviii, part ii, pp. 259–294.

1930. EYLES, V. A., in Economic Geology of the Ayrshire Coalfields, Area III (*Mem. Geol. Surv.*), pp. 139–143.

1930. BAILEY, E. B., and others, in The Geology of North Ayrshire (*Mem. Geol. Surv.*), pp. 263–264, 279–288.

1931. GUPPY, E. M., and H. H. Thomas, Chemical Analyses of Igneous Rocks, Metamorphic Rocks and Minerals (*Mem. Geol. Surv.*), pp. 73, 88.

1949. EYLES, V. A., J. B. SIMPSON, and A. G. MACGREGOR, in The Geology of Central Ayrshire (*Mem. Geol. Surv.*), Chapter X.

Fife.

1916. WALLACE, Mrs., Notes on the Petrology of the Agglomerates and Hypabyssal Intrusions between Largo and St. Monans, *Trans. Edin. Geol. Soc.*, vol. x, part iii, pp. 348–362.

1919. BALSILLIE, D., The Geology of Kinkell Ness, Fifeshire, *Geol. Mag.*, pp. 498–506.

1922. BALSILLIE, D., Notes on the Doleritic Intrusions of East Fife, *Geol. Mag.*, pp. 447–448.

1923. BALSILLIE, D., Further Observations on the Volcanic Geology of East Fife, *Geol. Mag.*, pp. 530–542.

1927. BALSILLIE, D., Contemporaneous Volcanic Activity in East Fife, *Geol. Mag.*, pp. 481–494.

1927a. BALSILLIE, D., East Fife Igneous Geology, *Proc. Geol. Assoc.*, vol. xxxviii, pp. 463–469.

1928. WALKER, F., and J. IRVING, The Igneous Intrusions between St. Andrews and Loch Leven, *Trans. Roy. Soc. Edin.*, vol. lvi, part i, pp. 5, 6, 15.

IX. TERTIARY DYKES

TERTIARY dykes with a general north-westerly trend are abundant in that part of the Midland Valley which lies south-west of a line through Greenock and Strathaven. In this area the majority of these dykes belong to a prolongation, south-eastwards from Cowal, of the Mull dyke-swarm. In the Midland Valley the breadth of this swarm approximates to at least twenty miles and may be as as much as thirty, for its south-western limit runs either near Troon or the Heads of Ayr. The dykes north-east of the Troon line are predominantly tholeiitic, with a few crinanites and allied olivine-dolerites and basalts. South-westwards from the neighbourhood of the Heads of Ayr crinanitic types are in the majority, and the dykes of this belt probably belong to a swarm connected with the Arran Tertiary volcano.

Tholeiitic Dykes. The great majority of the tholeiitic dykes are narrow (6 ft. to 10 ft. and occasionally 20 ft.) and individual examples can rarely be traced very far. These tholeiites are composed essentially of labradorite feldspar laths and augite, with varying amounts of mesostasis consisting of glass (or its devitrification products) darkened by iron-ore dust. Some contain in addition olivine, or phenocrysts of basic plagioclase feldspar (Tyrrell, 1917; MacGregor, 1930).

The most important members of the Mull swarm are, however, four broad (30 ft. to 120 ft.) dykes of somewhat different types which have been traced more or less continuously across the Midland Valley into the Southern Uplands (Plate VI). Two of these, the *Moneyacres–Hawick–Acklington dyke* and the *Cumbrae–Stevenston–Armathwaite–Cleveland dyke*, have been traced onwards to the east coast of England for distances totalling 130 and 180 miles. The other two, the *Barrmill–Muirkirk–Hartfell dyke* with the *Dalraith–Moffat–Eskdalemuir dyke* a little to the south-west of it, are situated between the Moneyacres and Cumbrae dykes, and close to the former; they also probably extend to the English coast, but are much less continuously exposed (MacGregor, 1930, 1949).

The big dykes, which vary considerably along their length in the proportion of mesostasis to feldspar and augite, have all been described as varieties of tholeiite, tholeiitic quartz-dolerite, or andesite. They may contain rhombic pyroxene and uniaxial augite, have a higher silica percentage (54 to 60 per cent) than the narrow tholeiitic dykes, and differ from the Permo-Carboniferous quartz-dolerites in their smaller grain-size and in other respects.

The *Cumbrae–Stevenston dyke*, the most acid of the group, is characterized by numerous phenocrysts of anorthite feldspar. From the Great Cumbrae, past Stevenston (near Saltcoats), and Barassie (near Troon) to Coylton (ten miles east of the Heads of Ayr) it has a south-easterly trend. Beyond Coylton it is seldom exposed, but appears to swing east-south-eastwards to the Southern Upland Fault, just beyond which (east of New Cumnock) a very similar dyke runs north-eastwards for some miles before resuming a south-easterly direction along the faulted north-eastern margin of the Sanquhar Coalfield. Here its south-easterly course is offset about ten miles to the north-east of the line Stevenston–Coylton–Armathwaite. It is believed, however, that the dyke splits near Coylton and that one branch extends with the normal south-easterly trend past Troston Loch (in the Southern Uplands) and Shearington (south-south-east of Dumfries) to Armathwaite in Cumberland (MacGregor, 1949, Fig. 18).

Another broad dyke (20 to 50 ft.) of distinctive type (a rather coarse tholeiitic quartz-dolerite) that has been traced intermittently, extends from Bracken Bay, at the Heads of Ayr, south-eastwards past Cairnhill and Straiton, and also changes its course north-eastwards near the Southern Upland Fault, which it crosses very obliquely. The north-easterly portion extends for over thirteen miles

G

to the Redree Burn. south-east of New Cumnock, where the dyke probably resumes a south-easterly course (MacGregor, 1949, Fig. 18).

The Tertiary age of the tholeiitic dykes is proved by their forming a prolongation of the Mull swarm. This deduction is supported by the fact that in the Midland Valley members of the swarm cut the Mauchline sandstones (Permian) a post-Coal Measures teschenite sill (Stevenston), Permian volcanic necks (p. 78) and an E.–W. Permo-Carboniferous quartz-dolerite dyke (Inverkip). In addition the Cleveland dyke in the north of England is known to be post-Jurassic.

Crinanitic Dykes. The majority of these dykes are fairly broad (20 ft. to 30 ft. and occasionally 60 ft.), and several have been traced for distances of one to three miles. The crinanites are composed of basic plagioclase feldspar, purplish augite, and olivine, with some analcite or zeolites and iron-ore (Tyrrell, 1917. 1920, 1923; MacGregor, 1930). Unlike the type crinanite dyke (Walker, 1934), they are often coarse-grained. Crinanitic dolerites or basalts with little or no analcite or zeolites are also common. Some of the coarse dykes (*e.g.* near Inverkip and Heads of Ayr) have alkaline felsic 'segregation' veins similar to those found in crinanite sills (*e.g.* Tyrrell, 1923).

The evidence for the Tertiary age of the N.W. to W.N.W. crinanitic dykes is much the same as in the case of the tholeiitic rocks. They occur either in the Mull or Arran Tertiary dyke-swarms and are known to cut the Mauchline sandstone. A dyke which probably belongs to the suite cuts a teschenite sill near Ardrossan (MacGregor, 1930). In Arran crinanitic dykes cut Triassic sandstones and are believed to be earlier than all Arran tholeiites.

SELECTED REFERENCES

1917. TYRRELL, G. W., Some Tertiary Dykes of the Clyde Area, *Geol. Mag.*, pp. 305–315, 350–356.
1920. TYRRELL, G. W., The Igneous Geology of the Ayrshire Coast from Doonfoot to the Heads of Ayr, *Trans. Geol. Soc. Glasgow*, vol. xvi, part iii, pp. 339–363.
1923. TYRRELL, G. W., Classification and Age of the Analcite-bearing Igneous Rocks of Scotland, *Geol. Mag.*, pp. 257–259.
1930. MACGREGOR, A. G., in The Geology of North Ayrshire (*Mem. Geol. Surv.*), pp. 289–315.
1931. GUPPY, E. M., and H. H. THOMAS, Chemical Analyses of Igneous Rocks, Metamorphic Rocks and Minerals (*Mem. Geol. Surv.*), pp. 52, 53, 77.
1934. WALKER, F., The Term 'Crinanite', *Geol. Mag.*, pp. 122–128.
1939. RICHEY, J. E., The Dykes of Scotland, *Trans. Edin. Geol. Soc.*, vol. xiii, part iv, pp. 419–425.
1942. ANDERSON, E. M., *The Dynamics of Faulting and Dyke Formation with Applications to Britain* (Oliver and Boyd, Edinburgh), pp. 41–53; 2nd Edition, 1951, pp. 43–58.
1949. MACGREGOR, A. G., in The Geology of Central Ayrshire (*Mem. Geol. Surv.*), Chapter XII.

X. MINERAL VEINS, ETC.

Mineral Veins. In the Midland Valley of Scotland mineral veins have in the past proved of economic importance in a few instances, but of late years the only ones that have been worked are barytes veins at the Gass Water Mines in Ayrshire and at Muirshiels Mine in Renfrewshire. Hematite (Auchinlongford and Garleton), barytes (Aberfoyle), galena, copper ores (Airthrey and Blairlogie) and native silver (Hilderstone and Alva) have all been worked locally in the past. The veins are usually found along faults or lines of crush; their age is probably Permian or/and Tertiary (MacGregor, 1944).

Graphite. In the Scottish coalfields graphite may locally be found to have developed from a coal seam where it is in contact with an intrusive dolerite sill. The only notable occurrence is at Craigman, some miles S.S.W. of New Cumnock, where a considerable amount of graphite was mined between the middle of the eighteenth century and the middle of the nineteenth (Clough, 1917; MacGregor, 1932).

SELECTED REFERENCES

Mineral Veins and Graphite.
1917. CLOUGH, C. T., in Special Reports on the Mineral Resources of Great Britain, Vol. V (*Mem. Geol. Surv.*), 2nd Edition, p. 29.
1920. FLETT, Sir J. S., in The Iron Ores of Scotland, Special Reports on the Mineral Resources of Great Britain, Vol. XI (*Mem. Geol. Surv.*), pp. 203, 209, 212.
1921. WILSON, G. V., The Lead, Zinc, Copper and Nickel Ores of Scotland, Special Reports on the Mineral Resources of Great Britain, Vol. XVII (*Mem. Geol. Surv.*), pp. 59, 60, 129, 140–145.
1922. WILSON, G. V., in Barytes and Witherite, Special Reports on the Mineral Resources of Great Britain, Vol. II (*Mem. Geol. Surv.*), 3rd Edition, pp. 97–112.
1930. SIMPSON, J. B., in The Geology of North Ayrshire (*Mem. Geol. Surv.*), p. 317.
1932. DINHAM, C. H., and D. HALDANE, The Economic Geology of the Stirling and Clackmannan Coalfield (*Mem. Geol. Surv.*), pp. 192–194.
1932. MACGREGOR, A. G., in Economic Geology of the Ayrshire Coalfields, Area IV (*Mem. Geol. Surv.*), p. 155.
1944. MACGREGOR, A. G., Barytes in Central Scotland, *Wartime Pamphlet No. 38* (*Geol. Surv.*).
1945. ROBERTSON, T., Scottish Mineral Deposits, in *Hydro-Electric Industries for Scotland* (Scottish Local Section of Institute of Metals, Glasgow), pp. 7–17.

Mineral Resources: General.
1940. MACGREGOR, M., and others, Synopsis of the Mineral Resources of Scotland, *Spec. Rep. Min. Res. Gt. Brit.*, Vol. XXXIII (*Mem. Geol. Surv.*) Includes water supply.

1945. MacGregor, A. G., The Mineral Resources of the Lothians, *Wartime Pamphlet No. 45 (Geol. Surv.).* Includes water supply.

1945. MacGregor, M., The Mineral Resources of Scotland, *Proc. Roy. Phil. Soc. Glasgow,* vol. lxx, part iii, pp. 27–42.

1946. Phemister, J., E. M. Guppy, and A. H. D. Markwick, Roadstone: Geological Aspects and Physical Tests, *Road Research: Special Report No. 3* (D.S.I.R.).

1951. Anonymous: Road Res. Lab. and Geol. Surv., Sources of Road Aggregate in Great Britain, *Dept. of Sci. and Indust. Research,* 2nd Edition.

See also Geological Survey Economic Coalfield Memoirs, Special Reports on Mineral Resources, and Wartime Pamphlets listed on p. 94.

XI. GLACIAL AND RECENT

Evidence of General Glaciation. During much of the Glacial Period Scotland was covered by an ice-sheet, many hundreds of feet in thickness, which completely buried even the highest hills. This ice-cover slowly moved outwards from the higher parts of the country, where it was renewed by precipitation. Owing to the pressure exerted by the moving ice, which soon became laden with rock-fragments in its lower parts, the subjacent rocks were ground away and the resulting debris was deposited as a widespread irregular sheet of ground-moraine. This stiff *boulder clay,* of very variable thickness (up to 150 ft. or more), still extends over the whole of the Midland Valley; only on steep hill-slopes, in the more elevated hilly tracts, and in post-Glacial river cuttings is the solid rock exposed.

The direction of ice movement has been deduced from a variety of evidence: (1) *The general alignment of scratches (striae) and grooves on ice-smoothed rock-surfaces;* (2) *The form of ice-moulded rock-knobs (roches moutonnées);* (3) '*Crag and Tail' formation:* where a mass of hard igneous rock surrounded by softer sediments was submerged under moving ice, it protected from erosion the softer rocks on its lee side. The volcanic plug of the Castle Rock, Edinburgh, with the long ridge of sedimentary rocks leading down eastwards to the Palace of Holyroodhouse, form one of the most perfect examples of 'crag and tail' in the Lothians, where this topographical form is particularly common; (4) *the direction of elongation of 'drumlins':* boulder clay covering the less elevated areas of sedimentary rocks is usually moulded into low hog-backed ridges ('drumlins') parallel to the direction of ice-movement. This type of scenery is characteristic, for instance, of the Ayrshire and Central Coalfields; (5) *The direction of carry of different types of boulder clay;* (6) *The nature of the stones and boulders in the ground-moraine:* boulders of distinctive types can be traced back to the rock-masses from which they were derived (*e.g.* the Lennoxtown essexite). The extension of Scandinavian ice across the North Sea to the east coast of Scotland is attested by occasional finds of typical Norwegian igneous rocks (*e.g.* rhomb-porphyry) on the Scottish mainland, as well as by the deflection of Scottish ice.

The main ice-trends may now be summarized. The confluence of ice moving southwards off the Highlands and northwards off the Southern Uplands produced in the central tract of the Midland Valley a general west to east ice-movement except in the area south-west of the River Clyde. Here, owing to the influence of the broad ridge of high ground that extends south-eastwards from the Firth of Clyde near Greenock (Plate I) the trend varied between a north to south and a north-east to south-west direction. Locally, during at least three distinct phases of the glaciation, successive ice-currents with very different trends were produced by variations in the pressure exerted by Highland, Southern Upland and Scandinavian ice.

In Kincardineshire, for instance, the evidence is partly supplied by the presence of superimposed boulder clays which differ in character owing to their divergent sources. During the first phase ice moving south-eastwards across Aberdeenshire was deflected by Scandinavian ice in the North Sea area and forced to take on a north-north-east to south-south-west trend across Kincardineshire. Near the coast the ground-moraine of this ice-sheet, being derived from the bed of the North Sea, is a black boulder clay containing marine arctic shells. During the second phase the effect of the North Sea Scandinavian ice was different, and an ice-sheet moving from south-west to north-east across the Lower Old Red Sandstone of Strathmore, and depositing a bright red boulder clay, was deflected *northwards* across eastern Aberdeenshire. The third phase is represented by a locally restricted south-easterly advance of Highland ice which did not every-where reach the coast. The ground-moraine of this ice sheet is grey in colour (Bremner, 1934; Campbell, 1934).

In northern Ayrshire three successive ice-trends have also been deduced. The evidence is as yet not nearly so satisfactory as in Kincardineshire and the time-relations between the movements of the two areas are unknown. During what is regarded as the first phase Highland ice moving southwards down the Firth of Clyde was deflected eastwards and deposited boulder clay containing marine arctic shells, such as *Astarte compressa*, *A. sulcata*, *Cyprina islandica*, at all levels up to 1,061 ft. There is also evidence of a second movement from north-east to south-west, and of a third from north-west to south-east (Bailey and others, 1930).

Interglacial Deposits. Evidence for an interglacial period (or periods) of milder climate has been recorded both in Kincardineshire and northern Ayrshire. The best-known localities, at Kilmaurs and the Cowdon Burn in Ayrshire, were discovered between 1815 and 1870. At Kilmaurs reindeer antlers and mammoth tusks, of which one at least is said to bear glacial striae, were found in an estuarine or fresh-water deposit intercalated in sandy beds containing marine arctic shells, the whole underlying boulder clay and resting on rock. At the

Cowdon Burn fossiliferous sedimentary beds, intercalated between two deposits of boulder clay, yielded a skull of *Bos primigenius* (wild ox), parts of antlers variously determined as *Megaceros hibernicus* (Irish 'elk') and *Cervus elaphus* (red deer), ribs of a small horse (*Equus caballus*), diatoms, desmidsa, beetles, ostracods, etc., and remains of mosses, birch, willow, Scots fir, etc. (Richey and Anderson, 1930). There has, however, been much controversy regarding both the Kilmaurs and Cowdon Burn deposits. In Kincardineshire a deposit of peat and silt, claimed as belonging to an interglacial period intervening between the first and second glaciations mentioned above, has recently been discovered at the Burn of Benholm (Campbell, 1934).

Effects of Ice-retreat. Throughout the protracted period during which the ice was disappearing on the approach of milder climatic conditions the abundant melt-waters produced notable local erosion and deposited the resulting debris over wide areas. The regional ice-sheet first disappeared from the higher ranges of hills,[1] such as the Lammermuirs, Pentlands, Ochils and Campsie Fells, but at this stage still covered much of the lowland areas, where its original thickness had been greatest. Melt-waters flowing between hill slopes and the marginal ice-cliffs of relict lowland ice locally formed temporary lakes with outlets (drainage channels) across the lowest available col. The glacial torrents cut well-marked marginal channels in boulder clay and rock, while the sand and gravel which they carried along were deposited in the temporary ice-dammed lakes and were often subjected to subsequent erosion when the ice dams gave way. Evidence for this sequence of events is provided: (1) by series of subparallel channels at successively lower levels (corresponding to stages in the retreat of the ice-fronts) many of which run almost along the contours, but some across spurs or cols[2]; (2) alluvial flats (terraces), moundy spreads (kames) and sinuous ridges (eskers) of sand and gravel found at varying elevations.

The most notable area where glacial retreat phenomena have been studied is on the northern flanks of the Lammermuir Hills (Kendall and Bailey, 1908; Bailey, 1910). Here a great series of marginal drainage channels flanking the higher ground is accompanied by extensive high-level and low-level deposits of sand and gravel. Similar phenomena have been studied in other areas, but full details of the retreat phenomena are not available for all districts. A satisfactory synthesis of the sequence of events has still to be worked out, although a preliminary attempt at broad generalization has been made by Charlesworth (1926).

The interpretation of the history of glacial drainage channels and fluvioglacial deposits, and time-correlations between different areas, are rendered difficult because local oscillations of the ice-fronts took place before the relict low-level ice became stagnant and finally disappeared.

---

[1] Valley glaciers probably pesisted locally, however, in these upland areas.
[2] Many of these channels arer now streamless ('dry valleys') but others have determined the course of existing streams.

A further difficulty is introduced by local evidence of large-scale late re-advances of Highland ice. The third ice-movement of Kincardineshire, mentioned above, was of this character and resulted in the formation of gravelly morainic accumulations, marking the limit of ice-readvance and stages in the final retreat, which were superimposed on earlier boulder clay that had undergone erosion.

Simpson (1933) has obtained detailed evidence of a late readvance of Highland ice (the 'Perth readvance') down the Teith valley and upper Strath Earn to form a 'Piedmont' glacier which reached the late-glacial sea in the Firth of Tay region. This glaciation was nurtured solely from the Grampian area. The limit reached by the ice during the Perth readvance, and the course of its retreat, are marked by extensive morainic and fluvio-glacial deposits and numerous marginal glacial drainage channels. Later and less extensive contemporaneous readvances of large glaciers from the Loch Lomond and Upper Forth valleys are indicated by well-marked gravelly terminal moraines in the Glen Fruin–Balloch–Drymen and Buchlyvie–Port of Menteith districts. The ground-moraine of the Loch Lomond glacier is richly charged with many species of arctic marine shells and it is clear that at the time of the initiation of this re-advance the sea extended northwards from the Firth of Clyde at Dumbarton into the Loch Lomond hollow, which was then free from ice, at least in its lower and middle reaches.

Raised Beaches.[1] The ice of the Perth and Loch Lomond readvances extended to the sea of late-glacial times, which stood at these periods somewhere between 65 ft. and 100 ft. above present-day sea-level (Simpson, 1933). This relationship, established by observed superposition of morainic deposits on marine or estuarine clays and silts, leads naturally to a consideration of the relics of terraces of marine alluvium (raised beaches) that fringe the open coastline on the east and west of the Midland Valley, and locally extend inland, especially from the large estuaries (Forth, Tay and Clyde). Particularly distinct terraces, often terminated on the landward side by old sea-cliffs, occur at about 100 ft. and 25 ft. above present-day sea level. In the Forth Valley they rise gradually to heights of about 150 ft. and 50 ft. respectively near Stirling (Dinham, 1927, 1932). Edinburgh and Glasgow are partly built on these beaches, which also form extensive 'carse lands' near Stirling and Perth. In the Forth and Tay valleys and elsewhere a peaty layer with remains of trees separates offshore (low-level) 100-ft. and (over-lying) 25 ft. beach deposits.

The explanation of these occurrences is as follows. It should be recalled first that observations on the depth of rock-head below superficial deposits in the valleys of the Forth and Clyde show that before the oncoming of the Glacial Period sea-level was at least 300 ft. or 400 ft. lower than at the present day (cf. MacGregor, 1940, 1942). The weight of the great Scottish ice-sheet depressed the

---

[1] We do not consider here the relative importance of rise and fall of the land and change in volume of the ocean in producing alterations in the level of the sea.

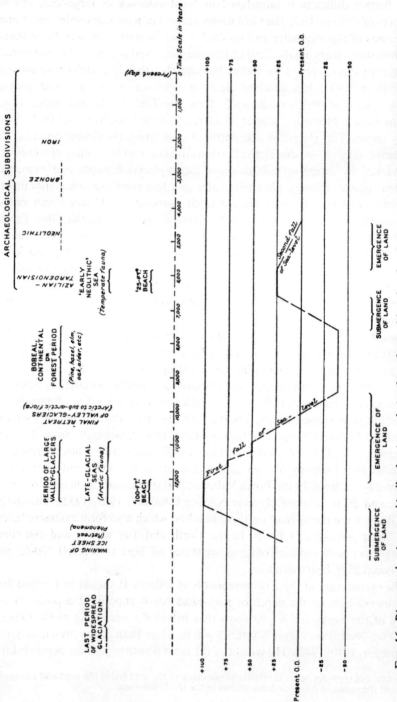

FIG. 16. Diagram showing graphically the time-relationship of raised beaches found at various levels around the coasts of the Midland Valley of Scotland

land until, towards the close of the Glacial Period, about the time of the final readvances of Highland ice, the sea stood somewhat over 100 ft. higher than now (Fig. 16). Along its shores, locally fringed by ice-lobes, sand and gravel were deposited. Offshore, in the larger estuaries, seasonally laminated silts and clays (varved clays) accumulated. On further deglaciation the land, relieved of its great load of ice, rose again and the sea receded, with minor pauses locally represented by raised beach-terraces, until well below its present level. Forests then flourished under milder climatic conditions (Boreal period). Subsequently the sea again encroached on the land until it stood for a considerable period about 25 ft. above its present level. Finally it retreated a second time and after minor oscillations the existing relative level of sea and land was established (Dinham, 1927; Callander, 1929).

In a number of bores and natural sections, both in the east and the west of the Midland Valley, beds of sand and gravel separate the arctic clays of 100-ft. beach age from the peaty layer that underlies 25-ft. beach deposits. They are probably fluvio-glacial sands and gravels formed during the uplift that inaugurated the Boreal period.

At various points on the coast there are relics of beaches at levels of approximately 50 ft. and 75 ft. (Fig. 16). These do not extend up the estuaries and appear to indicate minor halts in the post-Glacial emergence of the land.

Quite recently measurements of the varves (seasonal laminations) of 100-ft. beach clays have led to time-correlations of stages in the glacial history of Scotland and Scandinavia. Simpson has tentatively suggested that the Perth readvance is equivalent to the great Fenno-Scandinavian moraines south of Stockholm. These, according to De Geer's Swedish time-scale, belong to the beginning of the Finiglacial stage, and were formed almost 10,000 years ago. De Geer, however, using new measurements supplied by Simpson, correlates 100-ft. beach varves at Dunning in Strath Earn with a relatively early part of the Gotiglacial stage, which preceded the Finiglacial stage. According to this correlation the Dunning varves were formed rather more than 13,000 years ago.

The 100-ft. beach deposits contain shells of marine animals such as now live in Arctic and sub-Arctic waters. Common forms are *Chlamys (Pecten) islandicus, Cyprina islandica, Astarte borealis, Astarte compressa, Tellina (Macoma) calcarea*.

The 25-ft. or so-called 'Neolithic' beach (including the beach-carse at the 50-ft. level near Stirling) has yielded abundant temperate marine shells of present-day types such as cockles (*Cardium edule*), mussels (*Mytilus edulis*), oysters (*Ostrea edulis*) and periwinkles (*Littorina littorea*). *Scrobicularia piperata* is a common lamellibranch. Remains of seals and whales, 'kitchen-middens' (shell-heaps) and sporadic implements of early man (Azilian and late Tardenoisian) have also been found.

Recent Deposits. During and after the period of oscillation of land and sea level the rivers, readjusting themselves to form the modern drainage system, cut down through the fluvio-glacial sands and gravels, locally excavated deep gorges in boulder clay or rock, and in the major valleys formed alluvial terraces at successively lower levels.

Since the final stabilization of land and sea raised beach deposits have in many places been covered by dunes of wind-blown sand. Thick deposits of peat have accumulated on the carse-lands of the Forth and Tay, from which they have locally been removed by human agency (Cadell, 1913; Dinham and Haldane, 1932).

Since the end of the Glacial Period many of the numerous lakes left in hollows by the melting ice have shrunk or disappeared owing to the accumulation of silt, marl or peat, or to artificial draining. Diatomite deposits, occasionally found on Scottish lake sites (*e.g.* in Fife) have not warranted exploitation in the Midland Valley.

Economics. Fluvio-glacial deposits are extensively worked as a source of sand for moulding and for the making of mortar. The silts and clays of the raised beaches (especially those of the 100-ft. beach) and of dried up Glacial lakes and lakelets, have been employed in the manufacture of bricks, roofing tiles and field drains. In addition boulder clay is locally used for brick-making.

Low-level Midland Valley peat is used in drying malt for whisky manufacture, as bedding for horses, and in the making of fire-lighters.

SELECTED RFERENCES

1894. GEIKIE, J., *The Great Ice Age*, 3rd Edition (Stanford, London).
1898. SMITH, J., The Drift or Glacial Deposits of Ayrshire, *Trans. Geol. Soc. Glasgow*, vol. xi, Supplement, pp. 1–134.
1908. KENDALL, P. F., and E. B. BAILEY, The Glaciation of East Lothian south of the Garleton Hills, *Trans. Roy. Soc. Edin.*, vol. xlvi, part i, pp. 1–31.
1908. PEACH, B. N., in *Pentland Walks* (Edited by R. Cochrane; Pub. Elliot, Edinburgh), pp. 142–148. (Also later Editions.)
1909. PEACH, A. M., Boulder Distribution from Lennoxtown, Scotland, *Geol. Mag.*, pp. 26–31.
1910. PEACH, B. N., C. T. CLOUGH and others, in The Geology of the Neighbourhood of Edinburgh (*Mem. Geol. Surv.*), Chapter XVI.
1910. BAILEY, E. B., and others, in The Geology of East Lothian (*Mem. Geol. Surv.*), Chapter XVI.
1910. SAMUELSSON, GUNNAR, Scottish Peat Mosses, *Bull. Geol. Inst. Upsala*, vol. x, pp. 197–260.
1913. CADELL, H. M., *The Story of the Forth* (Maclehòse, Glasgow), Chapters VI and XIV.
1913. GREGORY, J. W., The Polmont Kame and on the Classification of Scottish Kames, *Trans. Geol. Soc. Glasgow*, vol. xiv, part iii, pp. 199–218.
1914. WRIGHT, W. B., *The Quaternary Ice Age* (Macmillan, London); 2nd Edition, 1937.
1923. READ, H. H., A. BREMNER and R. CAMPBELL, Records of the Occurrence of Norwegian Rocks in Aberdeenshire and Banffshire, *Trans. Edin. Geol. Soc.*, vol. xi, part ii, pp. 230–231.
1925. CARRUTHERS, R. G., and others in The Geology of the Glasgow District (*Mem. Geol. Surv.*), 2nd Edition, Chapter XI.

1926. CHARLESWORTH, J. K., The Readvance Marginal Kame-Moraine of the South of Scotland, and some later Stages of Retreat, *Trans. Roy. Soc. Edin.*, vol. lv, part i, pp. 25–50.

1926. GREGORY, J. W., The Scottish Kames and their Evidence on the Glaciation of Scotland, *Trans. Roy. Soc. Edin.*, vol. liv, part ii, pp. 395–432.

1927. DINHAM, C. H., Stirling District, *Proc. Geol. Assoc.*, vol. xxxviii, pp. 481–491.

1927. MACGREGGOR, M., Carstairs District, *ibid.*, pp. 495–499.

1928. WRIGHT, W. B., The Raised Beaches of the British Isles, International Geographical Union, *First Report of the Commission on Pliocene and Pleistocene Terraces*, pp. 99–106.

1929. ALLAN, D. A., The Glacial and Recent Drainage of the Lintrathen Area, *Geol. Mag.*, pp. 27–40.

1929. CALLANDER, J. GRAHAM, Land Movements in Scotland in Prehistoric and Recent Times, *Proc. Soc. Antiq. Scot.*, vol. lxiii, pp. 314–322.

1930. BAILEY, E. B., J. E. RICHEY, E. M. ANDERSON and A. G. MACGREGOR, in The Geology of North Ayrshire (*Mem. Geol. Surv.*), Chapter XXIV.

1932. DINHAM, C. H., and D. HALDANE, Economic Geology of the Stirling and Clackmannan Coalfield (*Mem. Geol. Surv.*), Chapter XII.

1932. DAVIDSON, C. F., The Arctic Clay of Errol, Perthshire, *Trans. Perthshire Soc. Nat. Sci.*, vol. ix, part ii, pp. 55–68.

1932. CHILDE, V. G., and MILES BURKITT, Chronological Table of Pre-history, *Antiquity* vol. vi, p. 185.

1933. SIMPSON, J. B., The Late-Glacial Readvance Moraine of the Highland Border west of the River Tay, *Trans. Roy. Soc. Edin.*, vol. lvii, part iii, pp. 633–646.

1933. MACGREGOR, M., and D. HALDANE, Economic Geology of the Central Coalfield, Area III (*Mem. Geol. Surv.*), Chapter IX.

1933. LINTON, D. L., The 'Tinto Glacier' and some Glacial Features in Clydesdale, *Geol. Mag.*, pp. 549–554.

1934. BREMNER, A., The Glaciation of Moray, and Ice Movements in the North of Scotland, *Trans. Edin. Geol. Soc.*, vol. xiii, part i, pp. 47–56.

1934. BREMNER, A., Meltwater Drainage Channels and other Glacial Phenomena of the Highland Border Belt from Cortachy to the Bervie Water, *ibid.*, pp. 174–175.

1934. CAMPBELL, R. On the Occurrence of Shelly Boulder Clay and Interglacial Deposits in Kincardineshire, *ibid.*, pp. 176–182.

1935. DE GEER, G., Dating of Late-Glacial Clay Varves in Scotland, *Proc. Roy. Soc. Edin.*, vol. lv, part i, pp. 23–26; see also *Trans. Geol. Soc. Glasgow*, vol. xix, part ii, pp. 335–339.

1935. MCCALLIEN, W. J., Dating the Ice Age in Britain, *Science Progress*, vol. xxx, pp. 67–71.

1935. ELDER, S., and others, ɪne Drumlins of Glasgow, *Trans. Geol. Soc. Glasgow*, vol. xix, part ii, pp. 285–287.

1937. MCCALLIEN, W. J., Rhu (Row) Point: a Re-advance Moraine, *Trans. Geol. Soc. Glasgow*, vol. xix, part iii, pp. 385–389.

1940. ANDERSON, J. G. C., Glacial Drifts near Roslin, Midlothian, *Geol. Mag.*, pp. 470–473.

1940. MACGREGOR, M., The Buried Channel of the Forth, *The Advancement of Science*, vol. i, No. 2 (*Rep. Brit. Assoc.*), p. 253.

1940. SIMPSON, J. B., and others, Discussion on the Raised Beaches of the Forth and Tay, *The Advancement of Science*, vol. i, No. 2 (*Rep. Brit. Assoc.*), pp. 254–256.

1942. MACGREGOR, M., The Leven Valley, Dumbartonshire, *Trans. Geol. Soc. Glasgow*, vol. xx, part 2, pp. 121–135.

1943. ANDERSON, J. G. C., *Scottish Sands and Gravels* (The British Limemaster Ltd., Tintagel).

1943. FRASER, G. K., Peat Deposits of Scotland: General Account, *Wartime Pamphlet No. 36, part* 1 (*Geol. Surv.*).

1948. ANDERSON, F. W., Fauna of the 100-ft. Beach Clays, *Trans. Edin. Geol. Soc.*, vol. xiv, part ii, pp. 220–229.

1949. SIMPSON, J. B., and V. A. EYLES, in The Geology of Central Ayrshire (*Mem. Geol. Surv.*), Chapters XIII and XIV.

1950. LACAILLE, A. D., The Chronology of the Deglaciation of Scotland, *Proc. Geol. Assoc.*, vol. lxi, part ii, pp. 121–144.

ADDITIONAL REFERENCES: GENERAL

1948. MACGREGOR, A. G., Problems of Carboniferous-Permian Volcanicity in Scotland, *Quart. Journ. Geol. Soc.*, vol. civ, pp. 133–152.

1948. ROBERTSON, T., Rhythm in Sedimentation and its Interpretation: with particular reference to the Carboniferous Sequence, *Trans. Edin. Geol. Soc.*, vol. xiv, part ii, pp. 141–175.

1948. ROBSON, D. A., The Old Red Sandstone Volcanic Suite of Eastern Forfarshire, *Trans. Edin. Geol. Soc.*, vol. xiv, part ii, pp. 128–140.

1949–51. WALTON, J., Various papers on Carboniferous plants, in *Ann. Bot.*, vol. 13, No. 52, 1949, pp. 445–452; *Trans. Roy. Soc. Edin.*, vol. lxi, part iii, 1949, pp, 719–736; *Trans. Geol. Soc. Glasgow*, vol. xxi, part ii, 1951, pp. 278–282.

1950. MOORE, R. A., Scottish Coal, *Scot. Geogr. Mag.*, vol. lxvi, No. 1, pp. 26–36.

1951. LINTON, D. L., Problems of Scottish Scenery, *Scot. Geogr. Mag.*, vol. lxvii, No. 2, pp. 65–85.

1951. PATTERSON, E. M., The Old Red Sandstone Rocks of the West Kilbride–Largs District, Ayrshire, *Trans. Geol. Soc. Glasgow*, vol. xxi, part ii, pp. 207–236.

1951. TYRRELL, G. W., A Boring through the Lugar Sill, *Trans. Geol. Soc. Glasgow*, vol. xxi, part ii, pp. 157–202.

1951. WESTOLL, T. S., The Vertebrate-bearing Strata of Scotland, *Internat. Geol. Congress, Rep. of* 18*th Session*, Gt. Brit., 1948, part xi, pp. 5–21.

1952. CLARK, R. H., The Significance of Flow-structure in the microporphyritic ophitic Basalts of Arthur's Seat, *Trans. Edin. Geol. Soc.*, vol. xv, pp. 69–83.

1952. COCKBURN, A. M., Minor Intrusions of the Pentland Hills, *Trans. Edin. Geol. Soc.*, vol. xv, pp. 84–99.

1952. DUNHAM, K. C., Age-relations of the Epigenetic Mineral Deposits of Britain, *Trans. Geol. Soc. Glasgow*, vol. xxi, part iii, pp. 395–429.

1952. KNOX, E. M., Palynology and Coal Stratigraphy, *Trans. Edin. Geol. Soc.*, vol. xv, pp. 221–233.

1952. TYRRELL, G. W., A second Boring through the Lugar Sill, *Trans. Edin. Geol. Soc.*, vol. xv, pp. 374–392.

1953. TOMKEIEFF, S. I., 'Hutton's Unconformity', Isle of Arran, *Geol. Mag.*, vol. xc, pp. 404–408.

1954. BENNISON, G. M., A new Species of *Carbonicola* from near the Base of the Namurian in Ayrshire, *Geol. Mag.*, vol. xci, pp. 32–44.

1954. NEAVES, W. D., The Microspore Content of the Chalmerston Coal, Dalmellington, *Trans. Geol. Soc. Glasgow*, vol. xxi, part iii, pp. 456–479.

1955. BENNISON, G. M., A *Myalina* fauna from the Namurian of North Ayrshire, *Geol. Mag.*, vol. xcii, pp. 448–456.

1955. PARKS, J. M. Jun., Variation in *Aulophyllum fungaites* from Petershill Limestone, Lower Carboniferous, Bathgate, West Lothian, Scotland, *Trans. Edin. Geol. Soc.*, vol. xvi, part ii, pp. 178–188.

1956. CLARK, R. H., A Petrological Study of the Arthur's Seat Volcano, *Trans. Roy. Soc. Edin.*, vol. lxiii, part i, pp. 37–70.

1956. HARRY, W. T., The Old Red Sandstone Lavas of the Western Sidlaw Hills, Perthshire, *Geol. Mag.*, xciii, pp. 43–56.

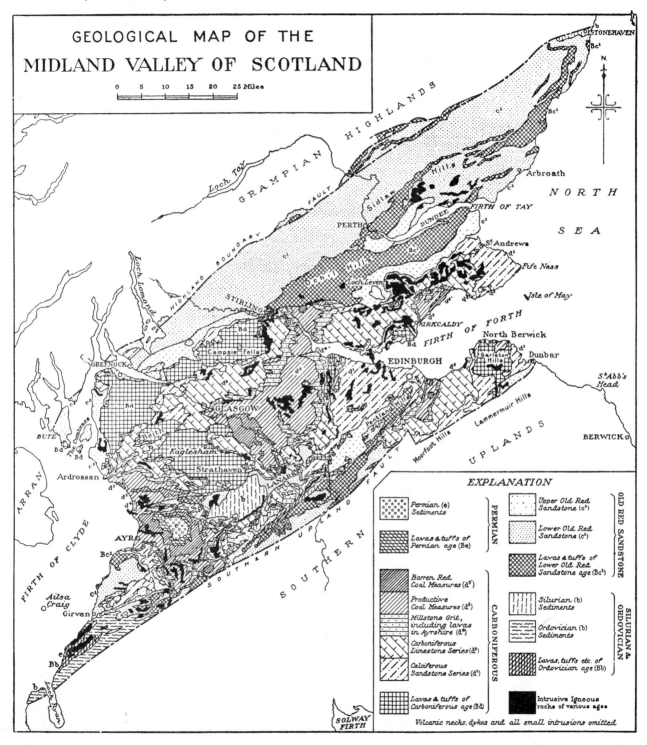

GEOLOGICAL MAP OF THE
MIDLAND VALLEY OF SCOTLAND

0   5   10   15   20   25 Miles

EXPLANATION

PERMIAN
- Permian (e) Sediments
- Lavas & tuffs of Permian age (Be)

CARBONIFEROUS
- Barren Red Coal Measures (d³)
- Productive Coal Measures (d³)
- Millstone Grit, including lavas in Ayrshire (d²)
- Carboniferous Limestone Series (d²)
- Calciferous Sandstone Series (d¹)
- Lavas & tuffs of Carboniferous age (Bd)

OLD RED SANDSTONE
- Upper Old Red Sandstone (c²)
- Lower Old Red Sandstone (c¹)
- Lavas & tuffs of Lower Old Red Sandstone age (Bc¹)

SILURIAN & ORDOVICIAN
- Silurian (b) Sediments
- Ordovician (b) Sediments
- Lavas, tuffs etc. of Ordovician age (Bb)

- Intrusive Igneous rocks of various ages

Volcanic necks, dykes and all small intrusions omitted

GEOLOGICAL SURVEY PUBLICATIONS[1] DEALING WITH THE MIDLAND VALLEY

(1) Maps

(a) *On scale of 4 miles to 1 inch: Colour-printed:*
Sheet 12. Perth, Brechin, Stonehaven, 1948.
„ 14. Stirling, Glasgow, Kilmarnock, 1948.
„ 15. Dunfermline, Edinburgh, Haddington, 1948.
„ 16. Ayr, Dalmellington, Girvan, 1948.

(b) *On scale of 1 mile to 1 inch:*
(i) *Colour-printed.*
Sheet 3. Stranraer, Portpatrick, 1923.
„ 7. Girvan, Ballantrae, Colmonell, 1926.
„ 8. Barr, Loch Doon, Carsphairn, 1929.
„ 14. Ayr, Mauchline, Dailly, 1933 (Solid, Drift and Soil Texture Editions).
„ 15. New Cumnock, Sanquhar, 1937 (Solid and Drift Editions).
„ 22. Kilmarnock, Troon, Dalry, 1928 (Solid, Drift and Soil Texture Editions).
„ 23. Wishaw, Carluke, Lanark, 1929 (Solid and Drift Editions).
„ 24. Peebles, Innerleithen, Biggar, 1932.
„ 30. Glasgow, 1958 (Solid Edition), 1961 (Drift Edition).
„ 31. Airdrie, Falkirk, Bathgate, 1924 (Solid and Drift Editions).
„ 32. Edinburgh, Midcalder, Queensferry. Solid Edition, 1930; Drift Edition, 1928.
„ 33. Haddington, Dunbar, 1910.
„ 40. Kinross, 1958 (Drift Edition), 1959 (Solid Edition).
„ 67. Stonehaven, 1929.
Glasgow District Map (parts of Sheets 30, 31, 22, 23), 1931 (Solid and Drift Editions).

(ii) *Hand-coloured.*
Sheet 13. Turnberry, etc. Solid Edition, 1902; Drift Edition, 1906.
„ 21. Fairlie, etc. Solid Edition, 1901; Drift Edition, 1906.
, 29. Wemyss Bay, etc., 1892.
„ 30. Paisley, Greenock, Dumbarton, 1878.
„ 38. Loch Lomond, Aberfoyle, Drymen, 1901.
„ 39. Stirling, Callander, 1882.
„ 40. Dunfermline, Leven, Kirkcaldy, 1898.
„ 41. Elie, North Berwick, 1889.
„ 47. Crieff, St. Fillans, 1888.
„ 48. Perth, Dundee, Cupar, 1883.
„ 49. St. Andrews, Arbroath, 1884.
„ 56. Blairgowrie, Kirriemuir, 1895.
„ 57. Forfar, Brechin, Montrose, 1897.
„ 57A. S.E. corner of Kincardineshire, 1881.
„ 66. Laurencekirk, Banchory, Aboyne, 1897.

(c) *On scale of 6 inches to 1 mile.*
Maps of the coalfield areas are also published on this scale in Drift and Solid editions.

[1] Stocks of Geological Survey publications were destroyed by enemy action. Those now on sale are listed in the latest edition of 'List of Geological Survey Maps' and of Government Publications Geological Survey and Museum: Sectional List No. 45.

(2) Memoirs

The Silurian Rocks of Britain: Vol. I, Scotland, 1899.

The Geology of Central and Western Fife and Kinross, 1900.

The Geology of Eastern Fife, 1902.

The Geology of the Neighbourhood of Edinburgh (Sheet 32, with part of Sheet 31). 2nd edition, 1910.

The Geology of East Lothian (Sheet 33, with parts of Sheets 34 and 41). 2nd edition, 1910.

Description of Arthur's Seat Volcano. 2nd edition, 1921.

The Geology of the Glasgow District (Parts of Sheets 30, 31, 22, 23). 2nd edition, 1925.

The Oil-Shales of the Lothians. 3rd edition, 1927.

The Geology of North Ayrshire (Sheet 22), 1930.

The Geology of Central Ayrshire (Sheet 14). 2nd edition, 1949.

The Geology of the Midlothian Coalfield, 1958.

Economic Geology of the Central Coalfield:
>   Area I. Kilsyth and Kirkintilloch, 1937.
>   Area II. Denny and Plean, Falkirk, Carron, Grangemouth, and Slamannan, 1917.
>   Area III. Bo'ness and Linlithgow, 1933.
>   Area IV. Paisley, Johnstone, and Glasgow, 1920.
>   Area V. Glasgow East, Chryston, Glenboig, and Airdrie. 2nd edition, 1926.
>   Area VI. Bathgate, Wilsontown, and Shotts, 1923.
>   Area VII. Rutherglen, Hamilton, and Wishaw, 1920.
>   Area VIII. East Kilbride, and Quarter, 1917.
>   Area IX. Carluke, Strathaven, and Larkhall, 1921.

Economic Geology of the Ayrshire Coalfields:
>   Area I. Kilbirnie, Dalry, and Kilmaurs, 1925.
>   Area II. Kilmarnock Basin, including Stevenston, Kilwinning, and Irvine, 1925.
>   Area III. Ayr, Prestwick, Mauchline, Cumnock, and Muirkirk, 1930.
>   Area IV. Dailly, Patna, Rankinston, Dalmellington, and New Cumnock, 1932.

The Ayrshire Bauxitic Clay, 1922.

Economic Geology of the Stirling and Clackmannan Coalfield, 1932.

Economic Geology of the Fife Coalfields:
>   Area I. Dunfermline and West Fife, 1931.
>   Area II. Cowdenbeath and Central Fife, 1934. 2nd edition, 1961.
>   Area III. Markinch, Dysart and Leven, 1954.

Special Reports on the Mineral Resources of Great Britain:
>   Vol. XI. The Iron Ores of Scotland, 1920.
>   Vol. XVII. The Lead, Zinc, Copper, and Nickel Ores of Scotland, 1921.
>   Vol. XXIV. Cannel Coals, Lignite, and Mineral Oil in Scotland, 1922.
>   Vol. XXXIII. Synopsis of the Mineral Resources of Scotland, 1940.
>   Vol. XXXV. The Limestones of Scotland, 1949.
>   Vol. XXXVII. The Limestones of Scotland, Chemical Analyses and Petrography, 1956.
>   Other volumes in this Series deal with Refractory Materials, Barytes, etc., for Great Britain as a whole.

Coalfield Papers of the Geological Survey of Great Britain.
>   No. 1. The Economic Geology of the Stirling and Clackmannan Coalfield, Scotland. Area North of the River Forth, 1956.
>   No. 2. The Economic Geology of the Stirling and Clackmannan Coalfield, Scotland. Area South of the River Forth, 1959.

Wartime Pamphlets:
   No. 5. Diatomite, 1940.
   No. 13. Limestones of Scotland:
      Area I. Southern Scotland, 1944.
      Area II. West Central Scotland, 1943.
      Area III. East Central Scotland, 1942.
   No. 24. The Limestone Coal Group of the Glasgow District, 1942.
   No. 27. The Oil-Shales of the Lothians: Structure:
      Area I. West Calder, 1942.
      Area II. Pumpherston, 1942.
      Area IV. Philpstoun, 1943.
   No. 36. Peat Deposits of Scotland: Part I. General Account, 1943.
   No. 38. Barytes in Central Scotland, 1944.
   No. 45. The Mineral Resources of the Lothians, 1945.

(3) Geological Photographs

See Classified Geological Photographs from the Collections of the Geological Survey and Museum, 1952.

Printed in Scotland for Her Majesty's Stationery Office.
Text by Jas. Deas & Son, Edinburgh. Cover and Art Section by Bell & Bain Ltd., Glasgow.
Dd 020014 K40